LEFT HAND GUITAR CHORDS MADE EASY

SEE IT HEAR IT

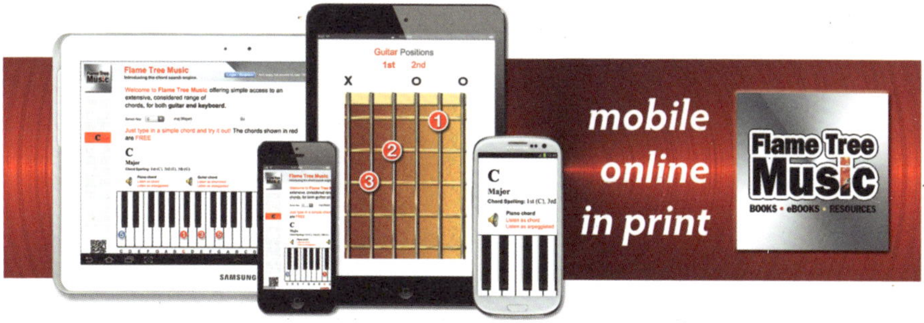

Publisher and Creative Director: Nick Wells
Project, design and media integration: Jake Jackson
Website and software: David Neville with Stevens Dumpala and Steve Moulton
Editorial: Laura Bulbeck, Emma Chafer and Esme Chapman

Special thanks to: Jane Ashley, Frances Bodiam, Helen Crust,
Christine Delaborde, Stephen Feather, Sara Robson, Chris Herbert, Polly Prior,
Gail Sharkey, Mike Spender and Birgitta Williams.

First published 2014 by
FLAME TREE PUBLISHING
Crabtree Hall, Crabtree Lane
Fulham, London SW6 6TY
United Kingdom

www.flametreepublishing.com

Music information site: www.flametreemusic.com

14 16 18 17 15
1 3 5 7 9 10 8 6 4 2

Every effort has been made to contact copyright holders. We apologize in advance for any omissions and would be pleased to insert the appropriate acknowledgement in subsequent editions of this publication.

The CIP record for this book is available from the British Library.

Android is a trademark of Google Inc. Logic Pro, iPhone and iPad are either registered trademarks or trademarks of Apple Computer Inc. in the United States and/or other countries. Cubase is a registered trademark or trademark of Steinberg Media Technologies GmbH, a wholly owned subsi[illegible], in the United States and/or other countries. Nokia's product names are either trademarks or registered trademarks of Nokia. Nokia is a registered trademark of Nokia Corporation in the United States and[illegible] and Galaxy S are both registered trademarks of Samsung Electronics America Ltd. in the United States and/or other countries.

Jake Jackson is a writer and musician. He has created and contributed to over 20 practical music books, including *Reading Music Made Easy*, *Play Flamenco* and *Piano and Keyboard Chords*. [illegible] available on iTunes, Amazon and Spotify amongst others.

ISBN: 978-1-78361-125-6

Printed in China

LEFT HAND GUITAR CHORDS MADE EASY

SEE IT HEAR IT

COMPREHENSIVE SOUND LINKS

JAKE JACKSON

Flame Tree Music

FLAME TREE
PUBLISHING

Contents

A
A♯/B♭
B
C
C♯/D♭
D
D♯/E♭
E
F
F♯/G♭
G
G♯/A♭

FREE ACCESS on smartphones including iPhone & Android

Using any QR code app scan and **HEAR** the chord (e.g. this is C Major).

Guitar Chords

An Introduction

Chords are the building blocks for every budding musician. Stringing together a few triads can liberate a melody and, being easy to communicate, will help you play with others. LEFT HAND GUITAR CHORDS MADE EASY combines a solid approach to chord diagrams with an integrated, online sound solution. There aren't too many books for the leftie but we hope this one helps fill the gap.

When I first started to play the guitar I bought a cheap steel-string acoustic, an **Epiphone**. I saw it in the window of a guitar shop I passed every day. It was surrounded by more glamorous instruments, mainly electric-blue **Fender Strats** and sunburst **Gibson Les Pauls**. But, at the price, I loved the look of it – the full body, the slim neck – and eventually saved up enough money to buy it, stealing myself for the inevitable complaints from my neighbours.

It didn't go well at first. In later years I came to realize that the cheaper the guitar, the harder they are to play, but at the time the strings were so far off the neck I could barely press them down and I suffered weeks of physical agony, nearly giving up. But I had a friend and he had a heavy wooden guitar, a beast, a **Westone Thunder**. I watched his impossibly big fingers float across the frets as he made the music dance, so he kept me inspired. And he was patient; oh, boy was he patient.

Eventually I *could* press down the strings, and continued with some simple chords, E minor, A minor, I think, and a top-three-string G major and a D major. Well, it's incredible how many songs can come from just these four chords! Of course I tried loads of chord books.

FREE ACCESS on smartphones including iPhone & Android

Using any QR code app scan and **HEAR** the chord (e.g. this is C Major).

A decent one is not ashamed of its reader because simplicity is essential at any level. You want to see the chord, understand it quickly and play it (I still do!). Of course the more you play, the more curious you get. And, when you're looking for new sounds, a new feel always comes from a new chord: it's very useful to explore the 6ths and the 9ths, and when your fingers are warm and loose, try some of the 7sus4s and 11ths, or 13ths. In the early days, I used to have a songwriting rule: ***every new tune would contain something new***, for me, sometimes it was a rhythm, sometimes a new verse/chorus structure, but most often, it was a **new chord**. Using a new set of notes can spring life into a tired bag of basic chords and force your developing musical brain into new territory.

So, chords are important to every songwriter, but especially for anyone playing with others, arranging and working out chord progressions. This new book offers just the first position on **20 chords per key**. It gives you a great range to experiment with and, combined with the power of mobile technology, you can **hear** how the chord is meant to sound by using a **smartphone** and any **free QR reader app**. Connected to the flametreemusic.com website you can hear each chord (on the piano and the keyboard) and a second guitar position too.

This is such a great tool, a unique experience that will give you hours of productive fun, whether you're bashing out some great songs, or playing with others. **Good Luck!**

Jake Jackson, London

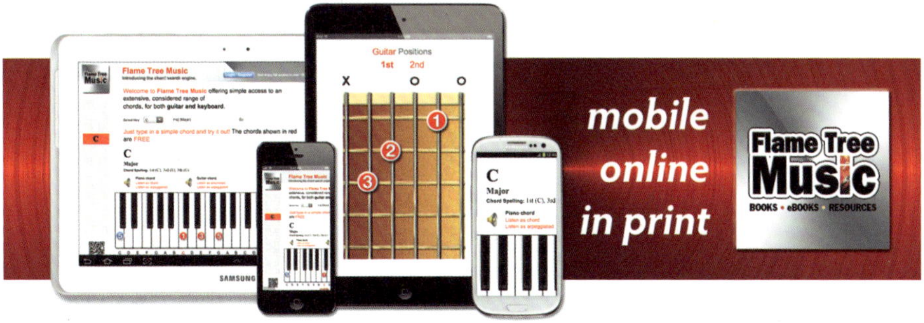

Chord Diagrams

A Quick Guide

The chord diagrams are designed for quick access and ease of use. You can flick through book using the tabs on the side to find the right key, then use the finger positions and fretboard to help you make the chord.

Each chord is provided with a *Chord Spelling* to help you check each note. This is a great way to learn the structure of the sounds you are making and will help with melodies and solo work.

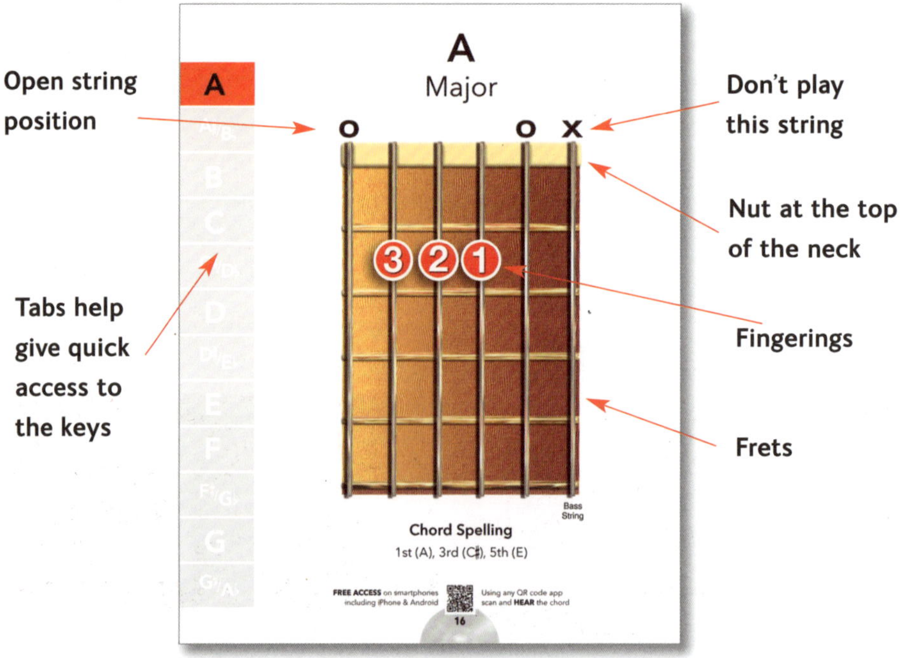
A
Major
A
Open string position
Don't play this string
O
O X
Nut at the top of the neck
3 2 1
Fingerings
Tabs help give quick access to the keys
Frets
Bass String
Chord Spelling
1st (A), 3rd (C♯), 5th (E)
FREE ACCESS on smartphones including iPhone & Android
Using any QR code app scan and HEAR the chord
16

FREE ACCESS on smartphones including iPhone & Android

Using any QR code app scan and **HEAR** the chord (e.g. this is C Major).

Title: Each chord is given a short and complete name, for example the short name C°7 is properly known as C Diminished 7th.

The Strings: The bass E appears on the right, the top E is on the left (The top E is the E above middle C on the piano).

E B G D A E

Fingerings:

❶ is the index finger
❷ is the middle finger
❸ is the ring finger
❹ is the little finger

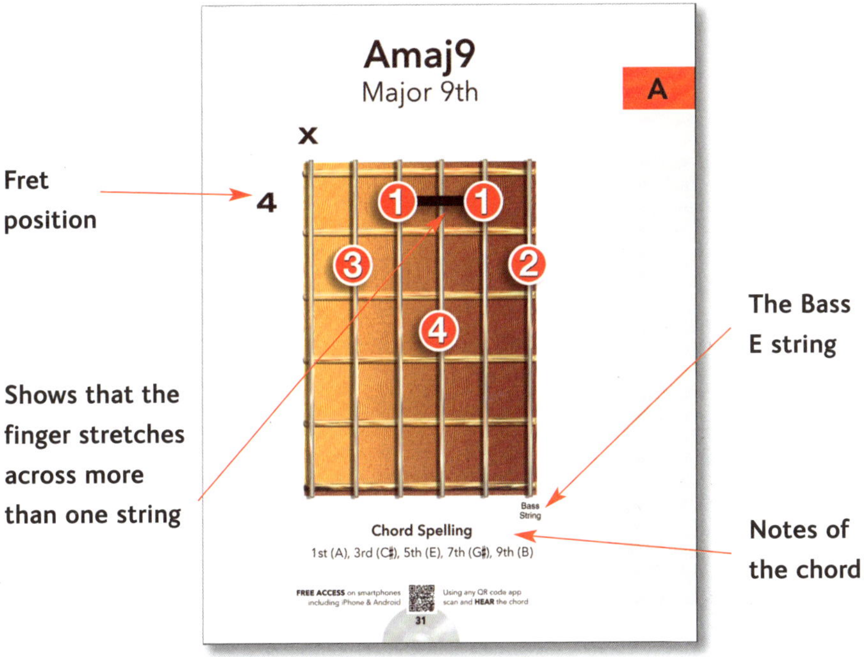
Amaj9
Major 9th
A
X
Fret position
4
1 1
3 2
4
Shows that the finger stretches across more than one string
The Bass E string
Bass String
Notes of the chord
Chord Spelling
1st (A), 3rd (C♯), 5th (E), 7th (G♯), 9th (B)
FREE ACCESS on smartphones including iPhone & Android
Using any QR code app scan and HEAR the chord
31

FREE ACCESS on smartphones including iPhone & Android

Using any QR code app scan and **HEAR** the chord (e.g. this is C Major).

The Sound Links

A Quick Guide

Requirements: a camera and internet ready smartphone (eg. **iPhone**, any **Android** phone (e.g. **Samsung Galaxy**), **Nokia Lumia**, or **camera-enabled tablet** such as the **iPad Mini**). The best result is achieved using a WIFI connection.

1. Download any **free QR code reader**. An app store search will reveal a great many of these, so obviously its is best to go with the ones with the highest ratings and don't be afraid to try a few before you settle on the one that works best for you. Tapmedia's QR Reader app is good, or ATT Scanner (used below) or QR Media. Some of the free apps have ads, which can be annoying.

2. Find the chord you want to play, look at the diagram then check out the **QR code** at the base of the page.

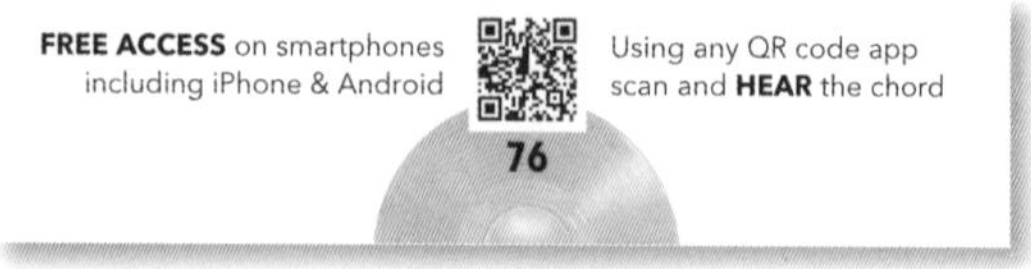

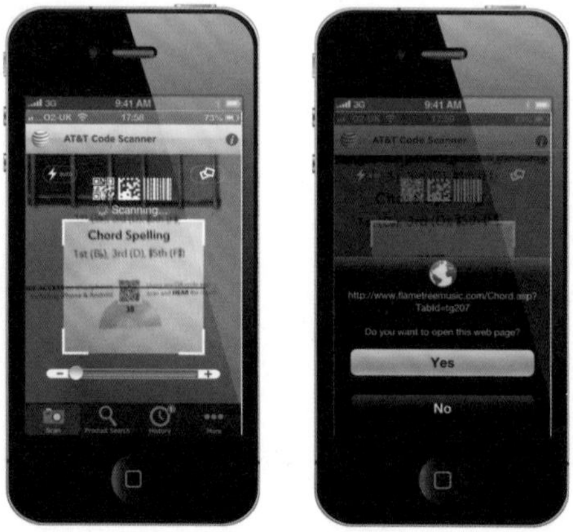

3. On your smartphone, open the app and **scan** the **QR code** at the base of any particular chord page.

4. The QR reader app will take you to a browser, then the specific chord will be displayed on the flametreemusic.com website.

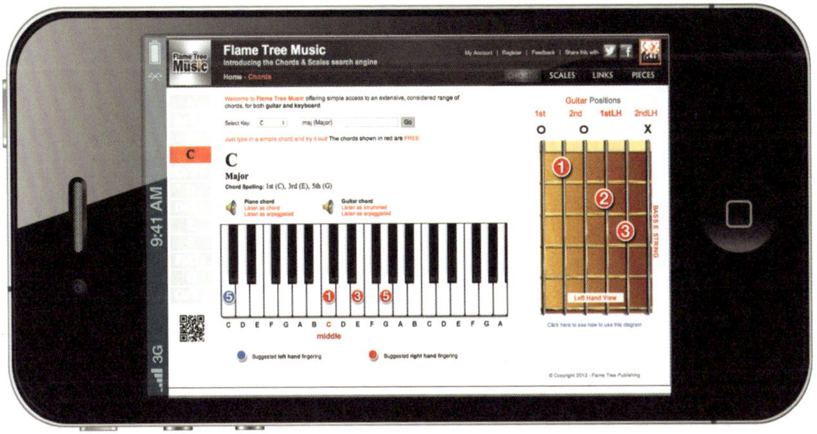

5. Using the usual pinch and zoom techniques, you can focus on four sound options.

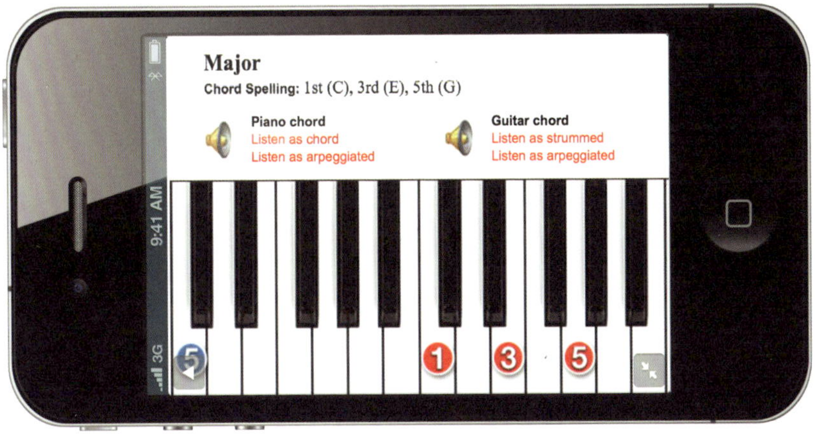

6. Click the sounds! Both piano and guitar audio is provided. This is particularly helpful when you're playing with others.

The QR codes give you direct access to all the chords. You can access a much wider range of chords if you register and subscribe.

FREE ACCESS on smartphones including iPhone & Android

Using any QR code app scan and **HEAR** the chord (e.g. this is C Major).

The Website

flametreemusic.com

The Flame Tree Music website is designed to make searching for chords very easy. It complements our range of print publications and offers easy access to chords online and on the move, through tablets, smartphones, desktop computers and books.

1. The site offers access to chord diagrams and finger positions for both the guitar and the piano/keyboard, presenting a wide range of sound options to help develop good listening technique, and to assist you in identifying the chord and each note within it.

2. The site offers 12 **free** chords, those most commonly used in a band setting or in songwriting.

3. A subscription is available for those who would like access to the full range of chords, **50** for **each key**.

FREE ACCESS on smartphones including iPhone & Android

Using any QR code app scan and **HEAR** the chord (e.g. this is C Major).

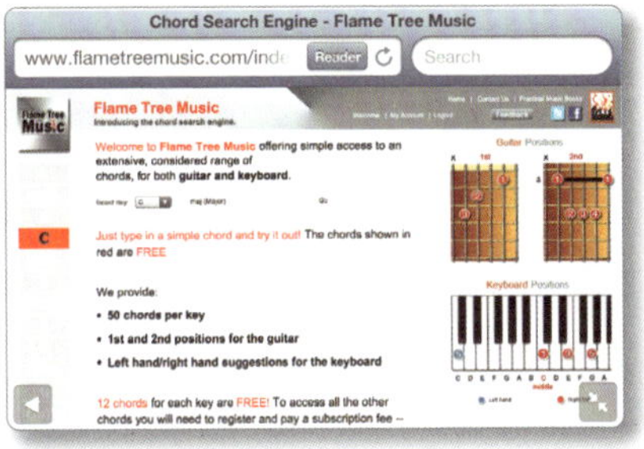

4. Guitar chords are shown with **first** and **second positions**, and **left-hand** options for each position.

5. For the keyboard, **left**- and **right-hand positions** are shown. The keyboard also sounds each note.

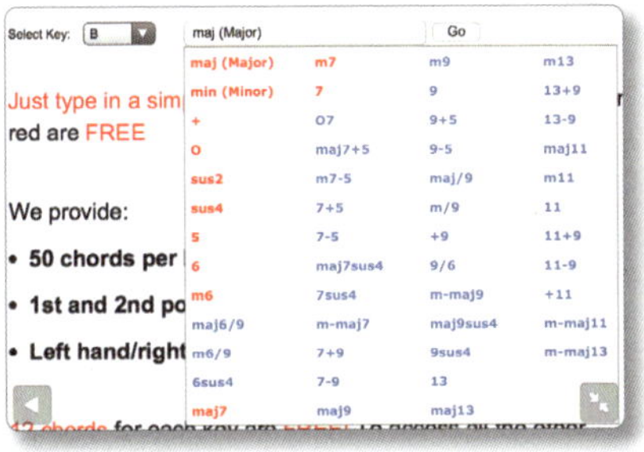

6. Choose the key, then the chord name from the drop down menu. Note that the **red chords** are available **free**. Those in blue can be accessed with a subscription.

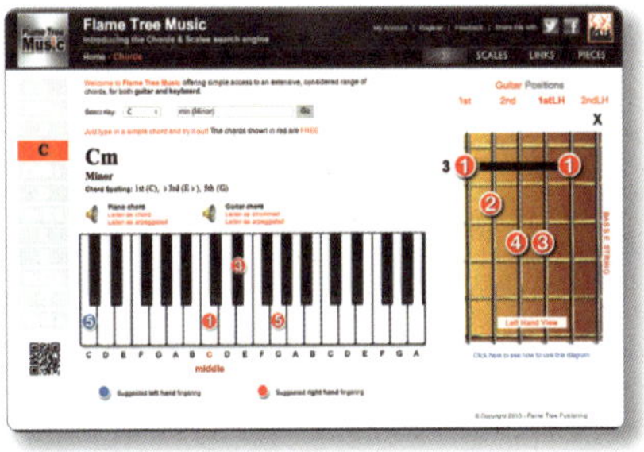

7. Once you've selected the chord, press **GO** and the details of the chord will be shown, with chord spellings, keyboard and guitar fingerings.

8. Initially, the first position for the guitar is shown. The second position can be selected by clicking the text above the chord diagram.

9. Sounds are provided in four easy-to-understand configurations.

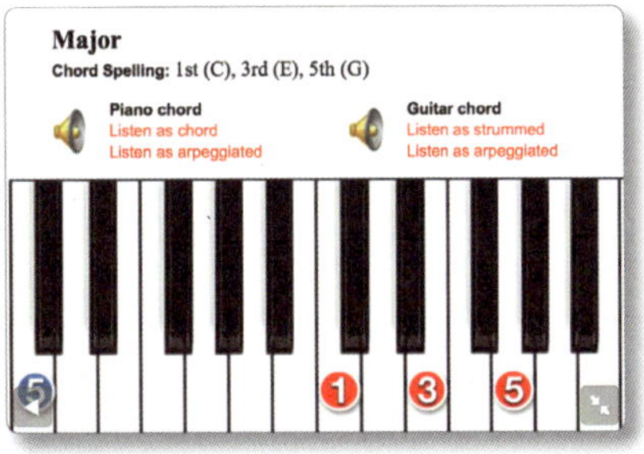

The website is constantly evolving, so further features will be added, including resources, scales and modes.

FREE ACCESS on smartphones including iPhone & Android

Using any QR code app scan and **HEAR** the chord (e.g. this is C Major).

The Chords

A
A♯/B♭
B
C
C♯/D♭
D
D♯/E♭
E
F
F♯/G♭
G
G♯/A♭

FREE ACCESS on smartphones including iPhone & Android

Using any QR code app scan and **HEAR** the chord (e.g. this is C Major).

A

A♯/B♭

B

C

C♯/D♭

D

D♯/E♭

E

F

F♯/G♭

G

G♯/A♭

A
Major

Chord Spelling

1st (A), 3rd (C♯), 5th (E)

FREE ACCESS on smartphones including iPhone & Android

Using any QR code app scan and **HEAR** the chord

Am
Minor

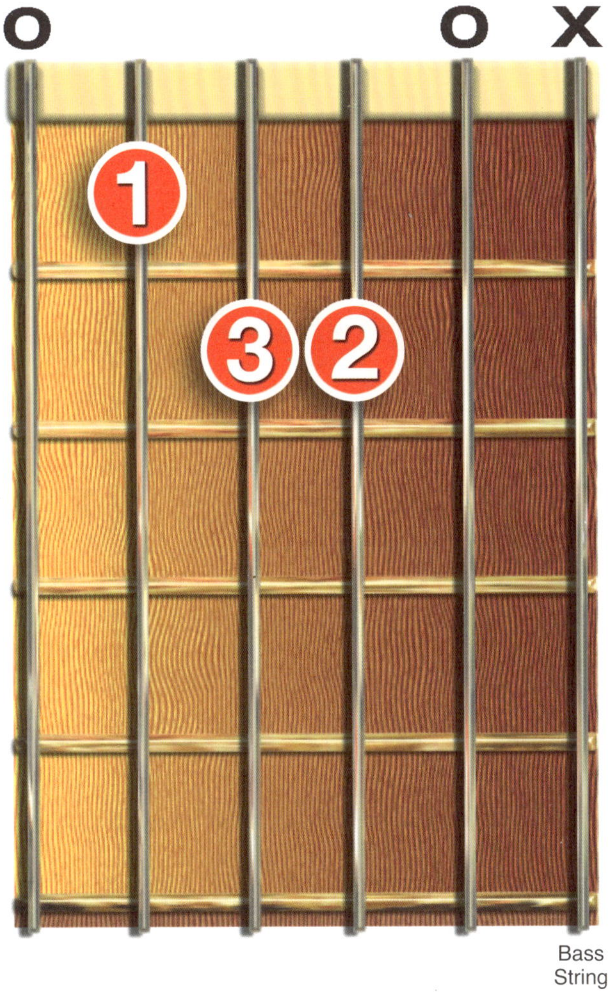

Chord Spelling

1st (A), ♭3rd (C), 5th (E)

FREE ACCESS on smartphones including iPhone & Android

Using any QR code app scan and **HEAR** the chord

A
A♯/B♭
B
C
C♯/D♭
D
D♯/E♭
E
F
F♯/G♭
G
G♯/A♭

A+

Augmented Triad

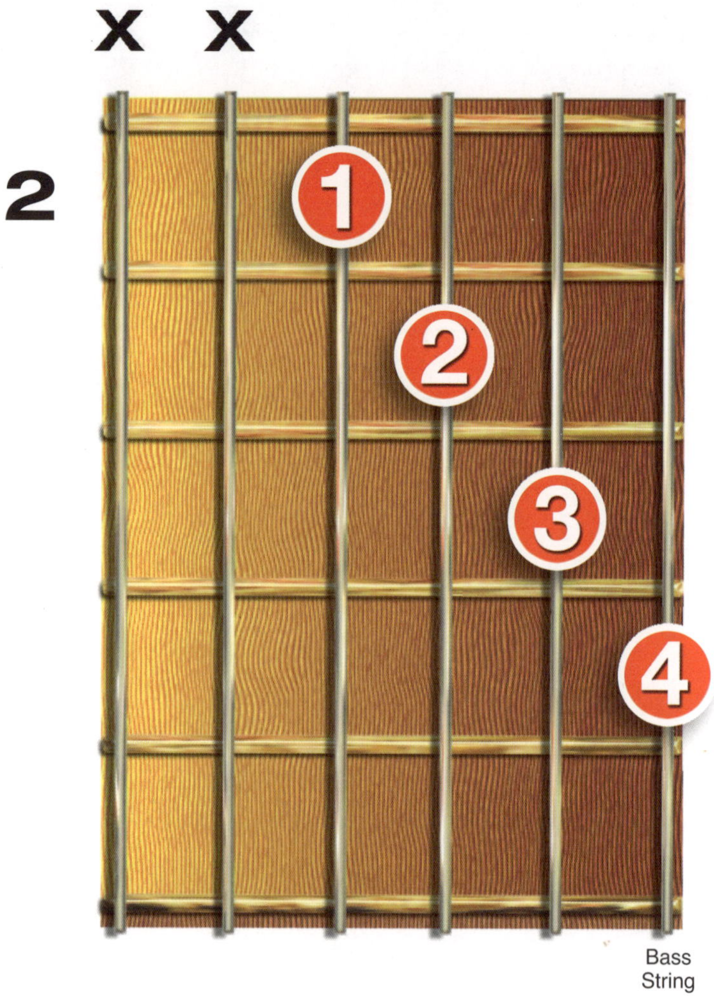

Chord Spelling

1st (A), 3rd (C♯), ♯5th (E♯)

FREE ACCESS on smartphones including iPhone & Android

Using any QR code app scan and **HEAR** the chord

A°

Diminished Triad

Chord Spelling

1st (A), ♭3rd (C), ♭5th (E♭)

FREE ACCESS on smartphones including iPhone & Android

Using any QR code app scan and **HEAR** the chord

Asus2

Suspended 2nd

Chord Spelling

1st (A), 2nd (B), 5th (E)

FREE ACCESS on smartphones including iPhone & Android

Using any QR code app scan and **HEAR** the chord

Asus4

Suspended 4th

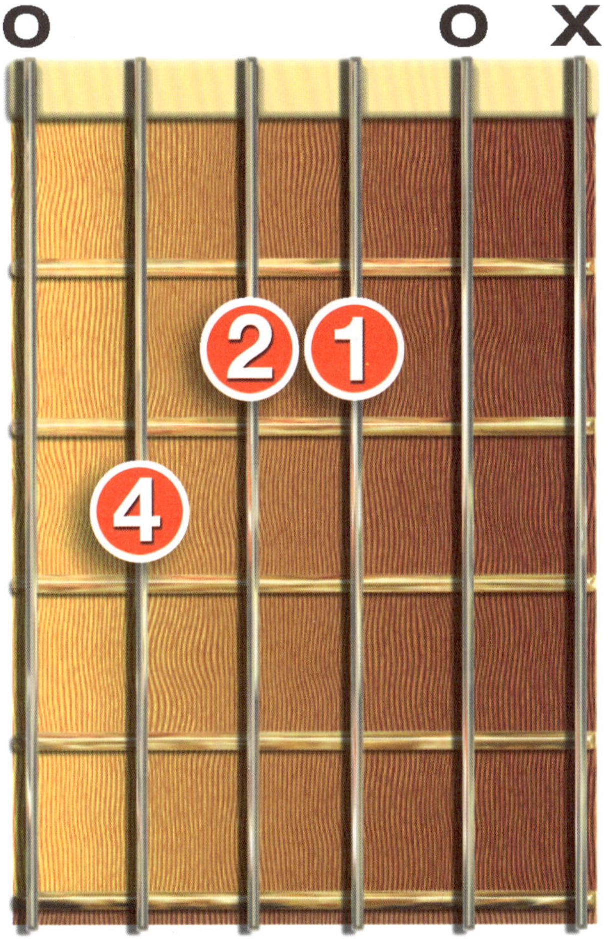

Chord Spelling

1st (A), 4th (D), 5th (E)

FREE ACCESS on smartphones including iPhone & Android

Using any QR code app scan and **HEAR** the chord

A5

5th (Power Chord)

X X O X
3
2
Bass String

Chord Spelling

1st (A), 5th (E)

FREE ACCESS on smartphones including iPhone & Android

Using any QR code app scan and **HEAR** the chord

A6

Major 6th

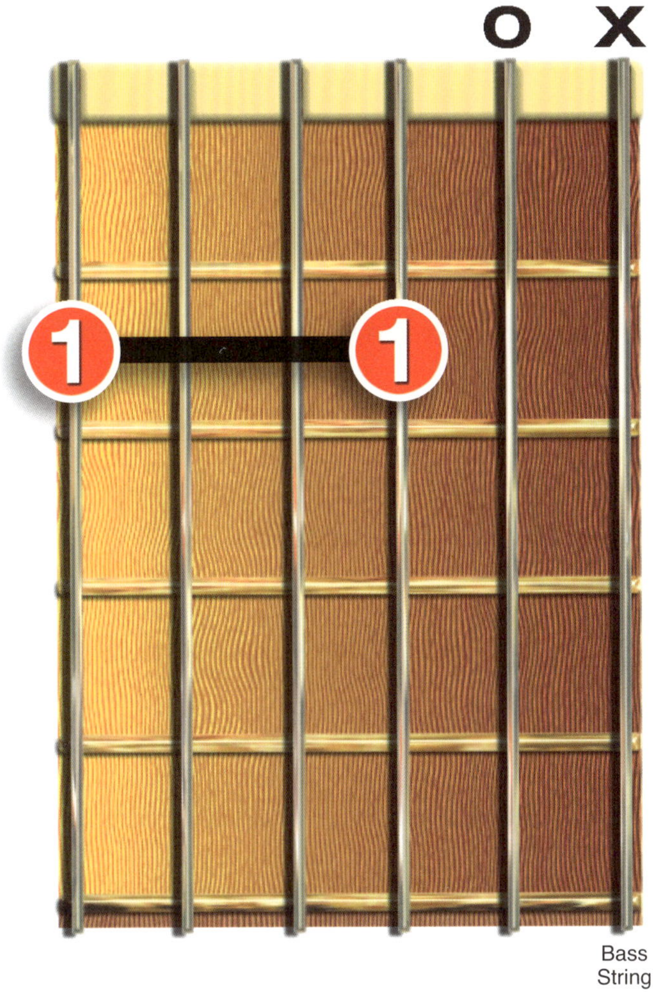

Chord Spelling

1st (A), 3rd (C♯), 5th (E), 6th (F♯)

FREE ACCESS on smartphones including iPhone & Android

Using any QR code app scan and **HEAR** the chord

A

A♯/B♭

B

C

C♯/D♭

D

D♯/E♭

E

F

F♯/G♭

G

G♯/A♭

Am6

Minor 6th

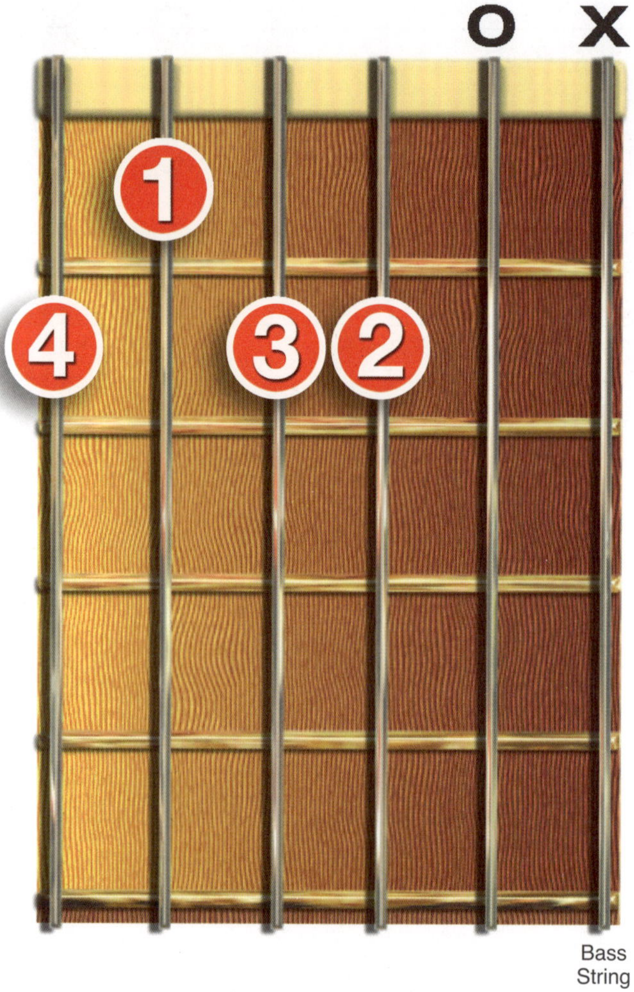

Chord Spelling

1st (A), ♭3rd (C), 5th (E), 6th (F♯)

FREE ACCESS on smartphones including iPhone & Android

Using any QR code app scan and **HEAR** the chord

A6sus4

6th Suspended 4th

Chord Spelling

1st (A), 4th (D), 5th (E), 6th (F♯)

FREE ACCESS on smartphones including iPhone & Android

Using any QR code app scan and **HEAR** the chord

A
A♯/B♭
B
C
C♯/D♭
D
D♯/E♭
E
F
F♯/G♭
G
G♯/A♭

Amaj7

Major 7th

Chord Spelling

1st (A), 3rd (C♯), 5th (E), 7th (G♯)

FREE ACCESS on smartphones including iPhone & Android

Using any QR code app scan and **HEAR** the chord

Am7

Minor 7th

Chord Spelling

1st (A), ♭3rd (C), 5th (E), ♭7th (G)

FREE ACCESS on smartphones including iPhone & Android

Using any QR code app scan and **HEAR** the chord

A7

Dominant 7th

Chord Spelling

1st (A), 3rd (C♯), 5th (E), ♭7th (G)

FREE ACCESS on smartphones including iPhone & Android

Using any QR code app scan and **HEAR** the chord

A°7

Diminished 7th

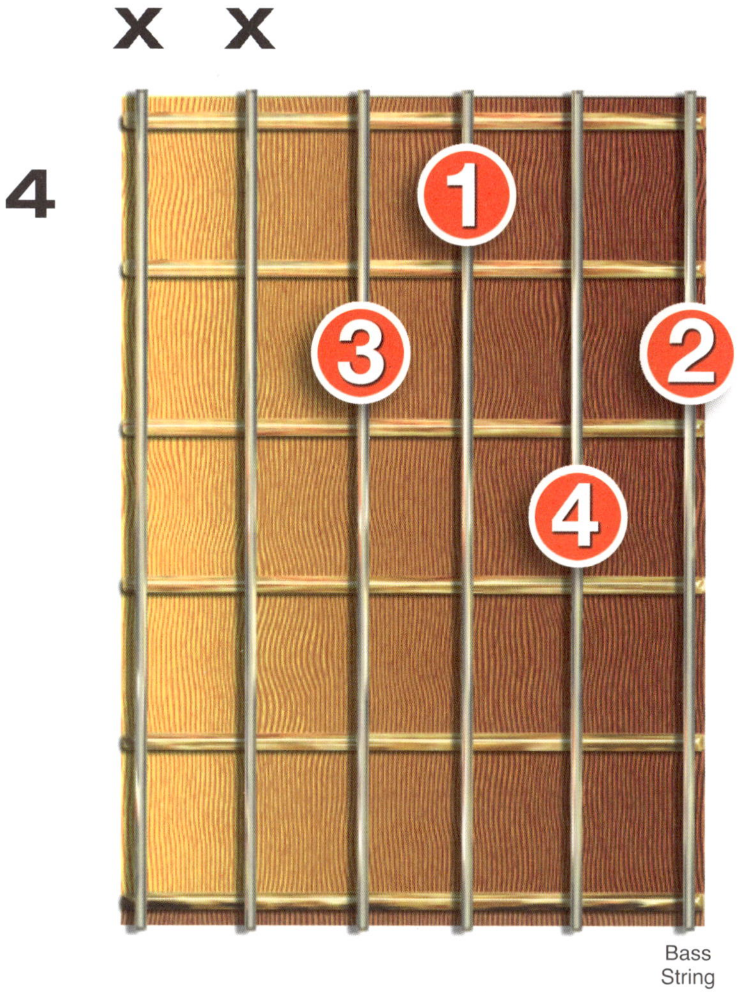

X X
4
1
3
2
4
Bass String

Chord Spelling

1st (A), ♭3rd (C), ♭5th (E♭), 𝄫7th (G♭)

FREE ACCESS on smartphones including iPhone & Android

Using any QR code app scan and **HEAR** the chord

A7sus4

Dominant 7th Suspended 4th

Chord Spelling

1st (A), 4th (D), 5th (E), ♭7th (G)

FREE ACCESS on smartphones including iPhone & Android

Using any QR code app scan and **HEAR** the chord

Amaj9
Major 9th

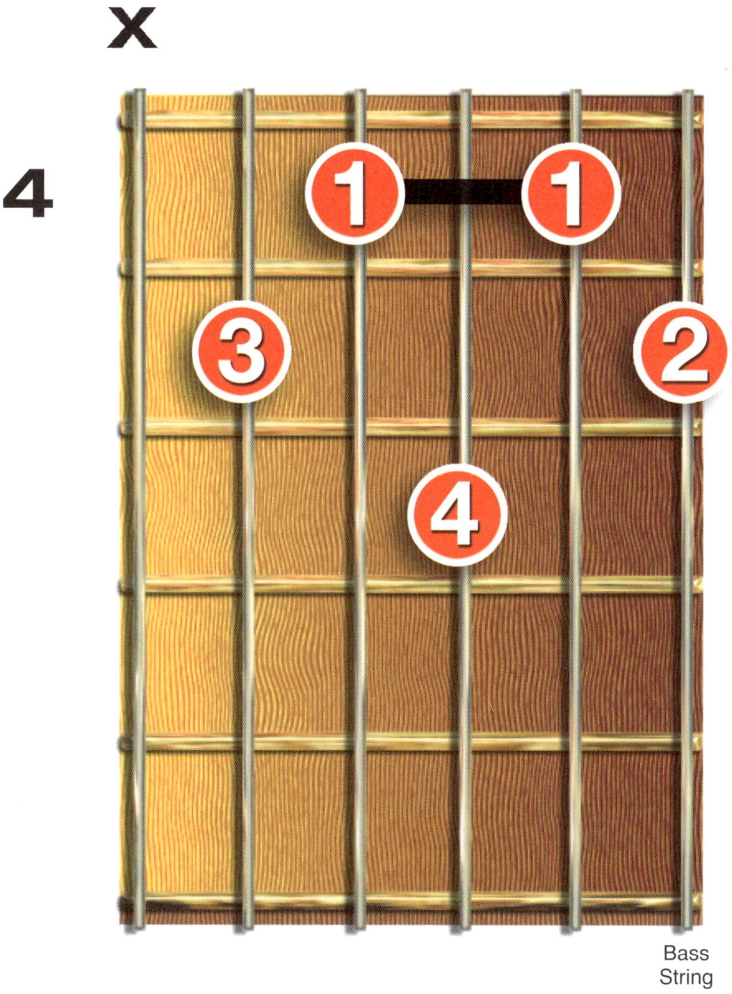

Chord Spelling

1st (A), 3rd (C♯), 5th (E), 7th (G♯), 9th (B)

Am9

Minor 9th

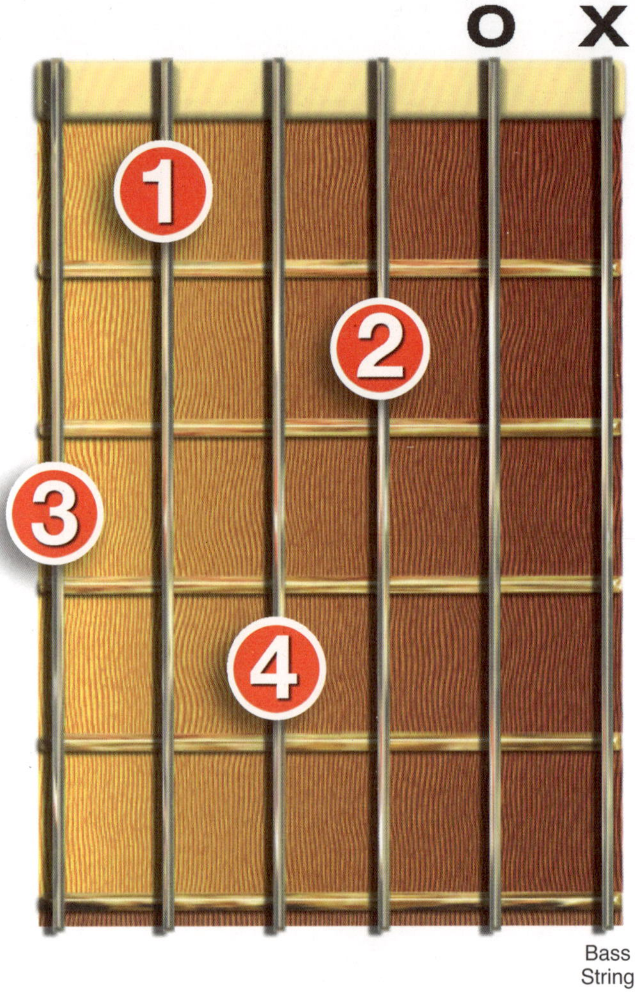

Chord Spelling

1st (A), ♭3rd (C), 5th (E), ♭7th (G), 9th (B)

FREE ACCESS on smartphones including iPhone & Android

Using any QR code app scan and **HEAR** the chord

A9

Dominant 9th

Chord Spelling

1st (A), 3rd (C♯), 5th (E), ♭7th (G), 9th (B)

Amaj11

Major 11th

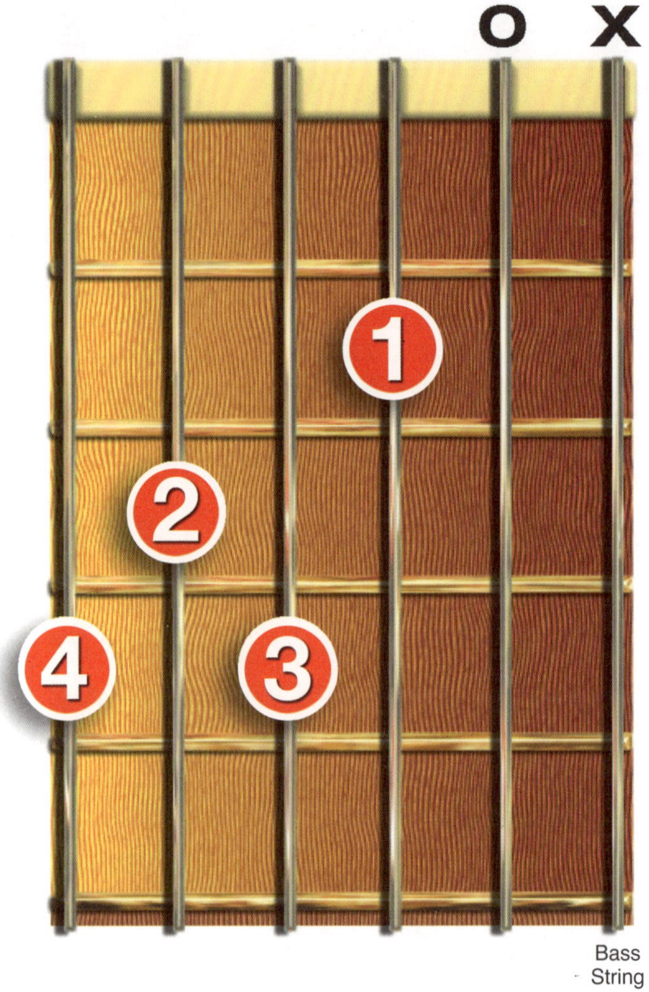

Chord Spelling

1st (A), 3rd (C♯), 5th (E), 7th (G♯), 9th (B), 11th (D)

FREE ACCESS on smartphones including iPhone & Android

Using any QR code app scan and **HEAR** the chord

Amaj13

Major 13th

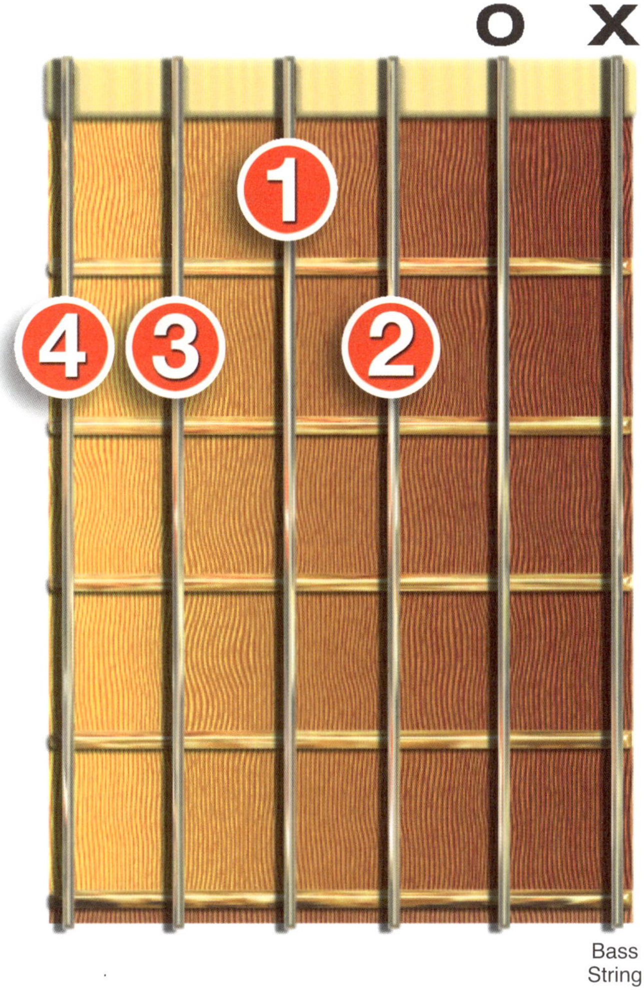

Chord Spelling

1st (A), 3rd (C♯), 5th (E), 7th (G♯), 9th (B), 11th (D), 13th (F♯)

FREE ACCESS on smartphones including iPhone & Android

Using any QR code app scan and **HEAR** the chord

A♯/B♭
Major

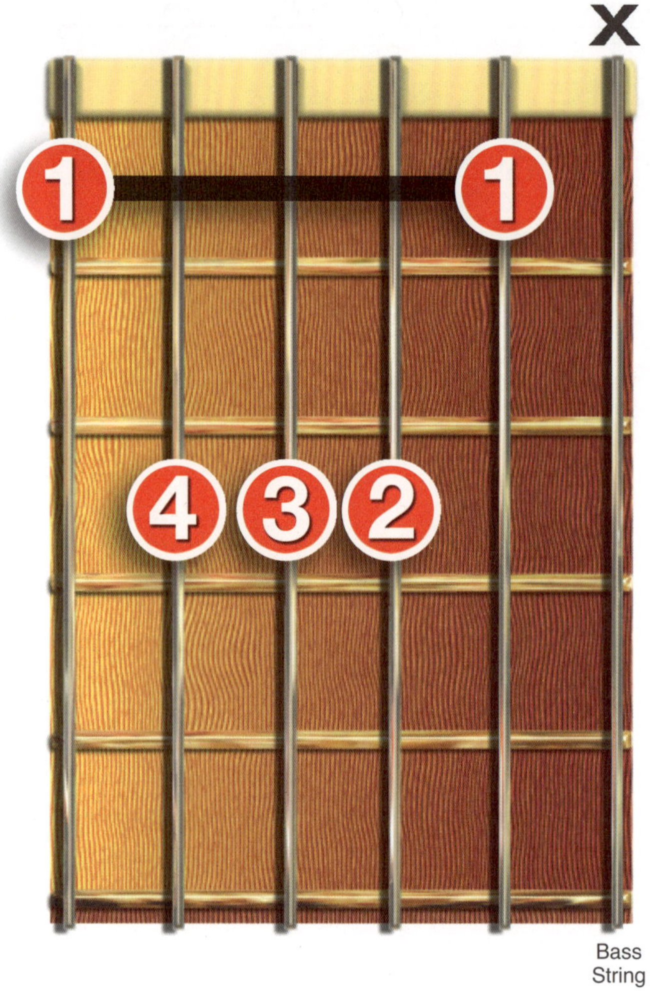

Chord Spelling

1st (B♭), 3rd (D), 5th (F)

FREE ACCESS on smartphones including iPhone & Android

Using any QR code app scan and **HEAR** the chord

A♯/B♭m
Minor

Chord Spelling

1st (B♭), ♭3rd (D♭), 5th (F)

FREE ACCESS on smartphones including iPhone & Android

Using any QR code app scan and **HEAR** the chord

A♯/B♭+
Augmented Triad

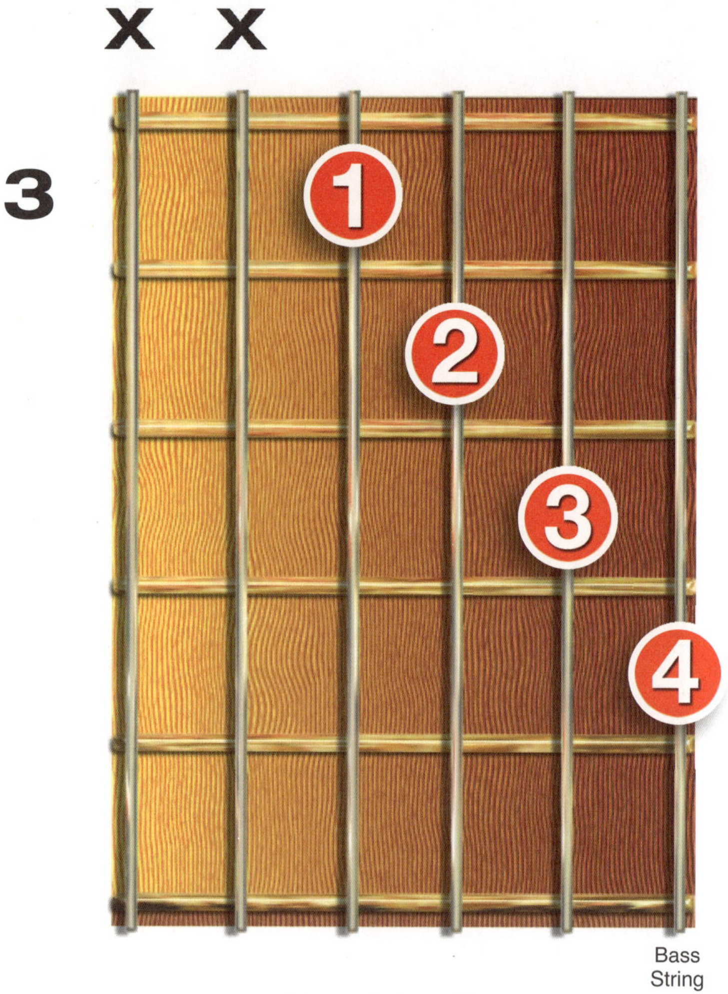

Chord Spelling

1st (B♭), 3rd (D), ♯5th (F♯)

FREE ACCESS on smartphones including iPhone & Android

Using any QR code app scan and **HEAR** the chord

A♯/B♭°
Diminished Triad

Chord Spelling

1st (B♭), ♭3rd (D♭), ♭5th (F♭)

A♯/B♭sus2
Suspended 2nd

Chord Spelling

1st (B♭), 2nd (C), 5th (F)

FREE ACCESS on smartphones including iPhone & Android

Using any QR code app scan and **HEAR** the chord

A♯/B♭sus4

Suspended 4th

Chord Spelling

1st (B♭), 4th (E♭), 5th (F)

FREE ACCESS on smartphones including iPhone & Android

Using any QR code app scan and **HEAR** the chord

A♯/B♭5
5th (Power Chord)

Chord Spelling

1st (B♭), 5th (F)

FREE ACCESS on smartphones including iPhone & Android

Using any QR code app scan and **HEAR** the chord

A♯/B♭6
Major 6th

Chord Spelling

1st (B♭), 3rd (D), 5th (F), 6th (G)

FREE ACCESS on smartphones including iPhone & Android

Using any QR code app scan and **HEAR** the chord

A♯/B♭m6

Minor 6th

Chord Spelling

1st (B♭), ♭3rd (D♭), 5th (F), 6th (G)

FREE ACCESS on smartphones including iPhone & Android

Using any QR code app scan and **HEAR** the chord

A♯/B♭6sus4

6th Suspended 4th

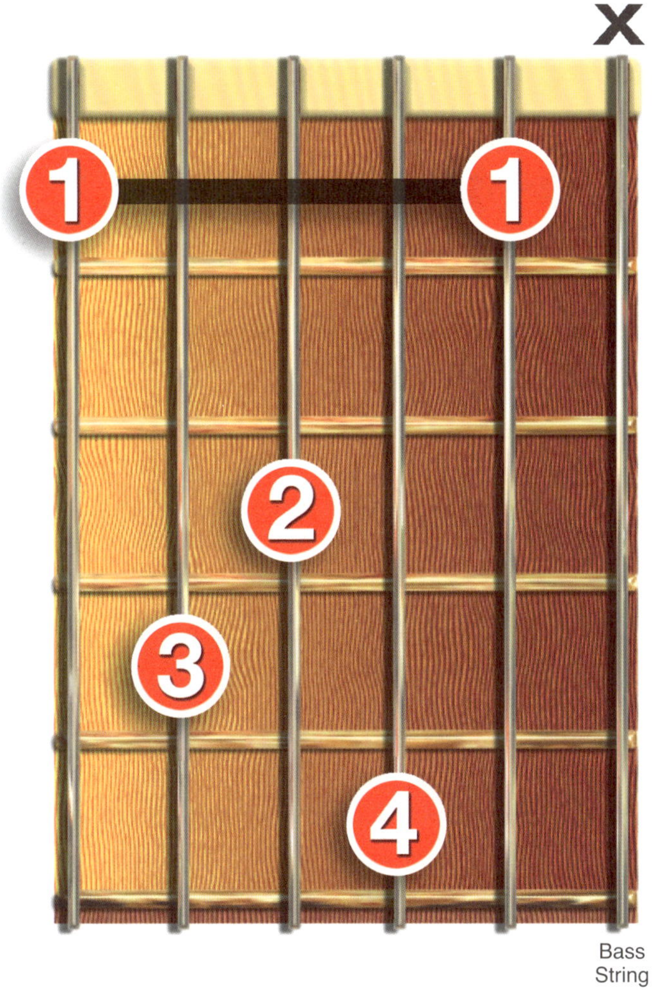

Chord Spelling

1st (B♭), 4th (E♭), 5th (F), 6th (G)

FREE ACCESS on smartphones including iPhone & Android

Using any QR code app scan and **HEAR** the chord

A♯/B♭maj7

Major 7th

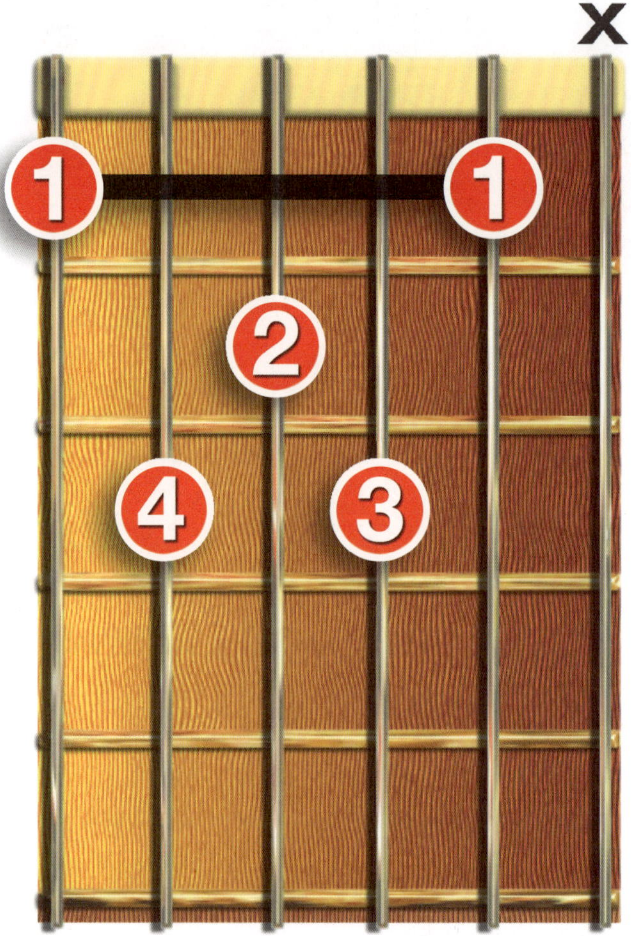

Chord Spelling

1st (B♭), 3rd (D), 5th (F), 7th (A)

FREE ACCESS on smartphones including iPhone & Android

Using any QR code app scan and **HEAR** the chord

A♯/B♭m7

Minor 7th

Chord Spelling

1st (B♭), ♭3rd (D♭), 5th (F), ♭7th (A♭)

FREE ACCESS on smartphones including iPhone & Android

Using any QR code app scan and **HEAR** the chord

A♯/B♭7

Dominant 7th

Chord Spelling

1st (B♭), 3rd (D), 5th (F), ♭7th (A♭)

FREE ACCESS on smartphones including iPhone & Android

Using any QR code app scan and **HEAR** the chord

A♯/B♭°7

Diminished 7th

Chord Spelling

1st (B♭), ♭3rd (D♭), ♭5th (F♭), 𝄫7th (A𝄫)

FREE ACCESS on smartphones including iPhone & Android

Using any QR code app scan and **HEAR** the chord

A
A♯/B♭
B
C
C♯/D♭
D
D♯/E♭
E
F
F♯/G♭
G
G♯/A♭

A♯/B♭7sus4

Dominant 7th Suspended 4th

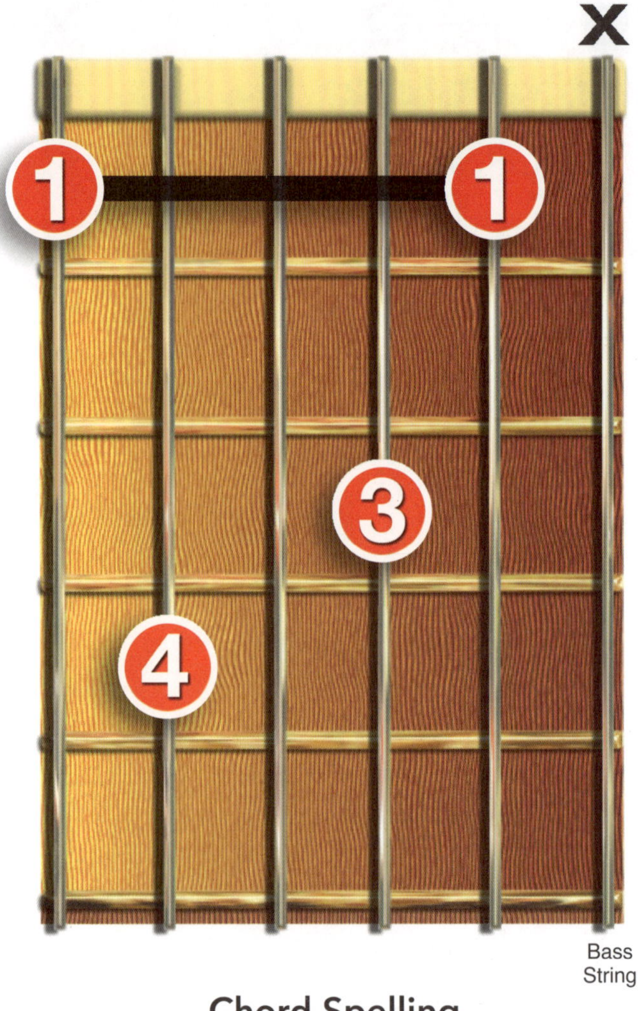

Chord Spelling

1st (B♭), 4th (E♭), 5th (F), ♭7th (A♭)

FREE ACCESS on smartphones including iPhone & Android

Using any QR code app scan and **HEAR** the chord

A♯/B♭maj9
Major 9th

Chord Spelling

1st (B♭), 3rd (D), 5th (F), 7th (A), 9th (C)

A
A♯/B♭
B
C
C♯/D♭
D
D♯/E♭
E
F
F♯/G♭
G
G♯/A♭

A♯/B♭m9

Minor 9th

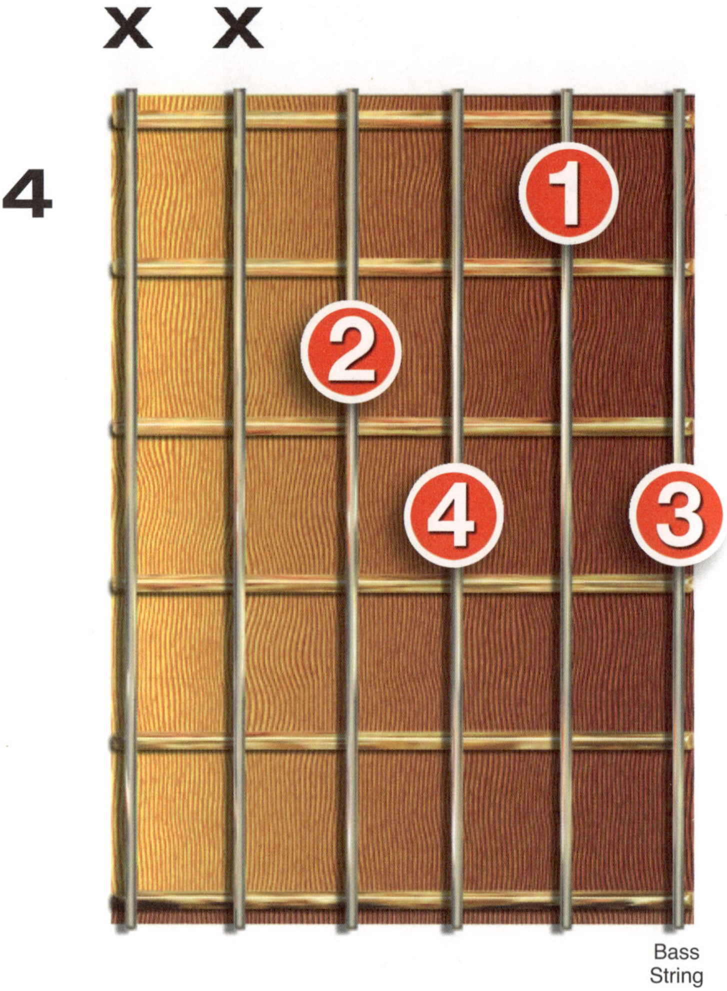
x
x
4
1
2
4
3
Bass
String

Chord Spelling

1st (B♭), ♭3rd (D♭), 5th (F), ♭7th (A♭), 9th (C)

FREE ACCESS on smartphones including iPhone & Android

Using any QR code app scan and **HEAR** the chord

A♯/B♭9

Dominant 9th

Chord Spelling

1st (B♭), 3rd (D), 5th (F), ♭7th (A♭), 9th (C)

FREE ACCESS on smartphones including iPhone & Android

Using any QR code app scan and **HEAR** the chord

A♯/B♭maj11

Major 11th

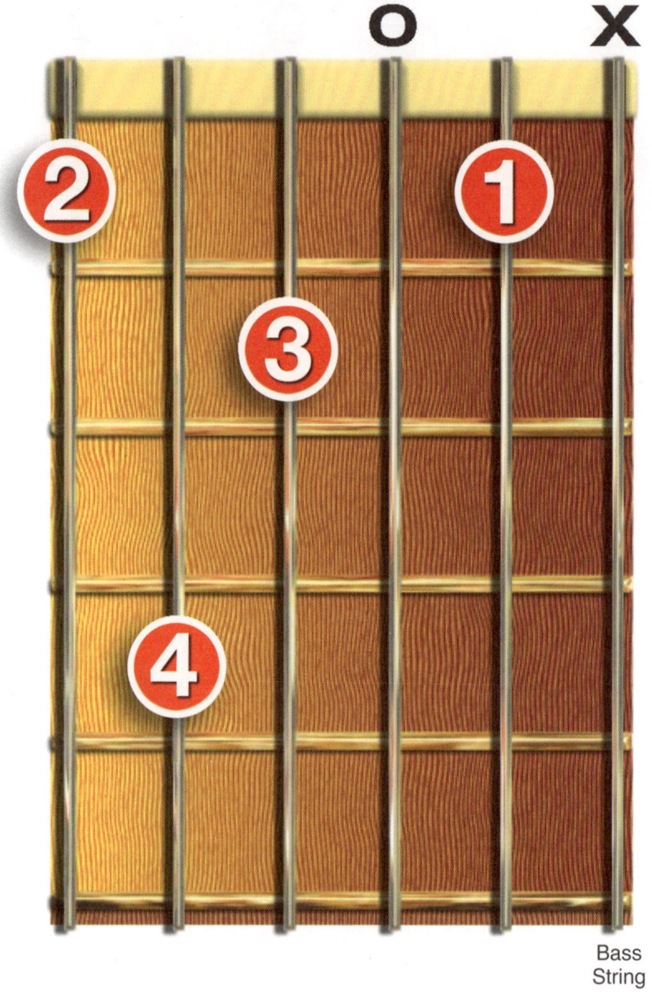

Chord Spelling

1st (B♭), 3rd (D), 5th (F), 7th (A), 9th (C), 11th (E♭)

FREE ACCESS on smartphones including iPhone & Android

Using any QR code app scan and **HEAR** the chord

A♯/B♭maj13

Major 13th

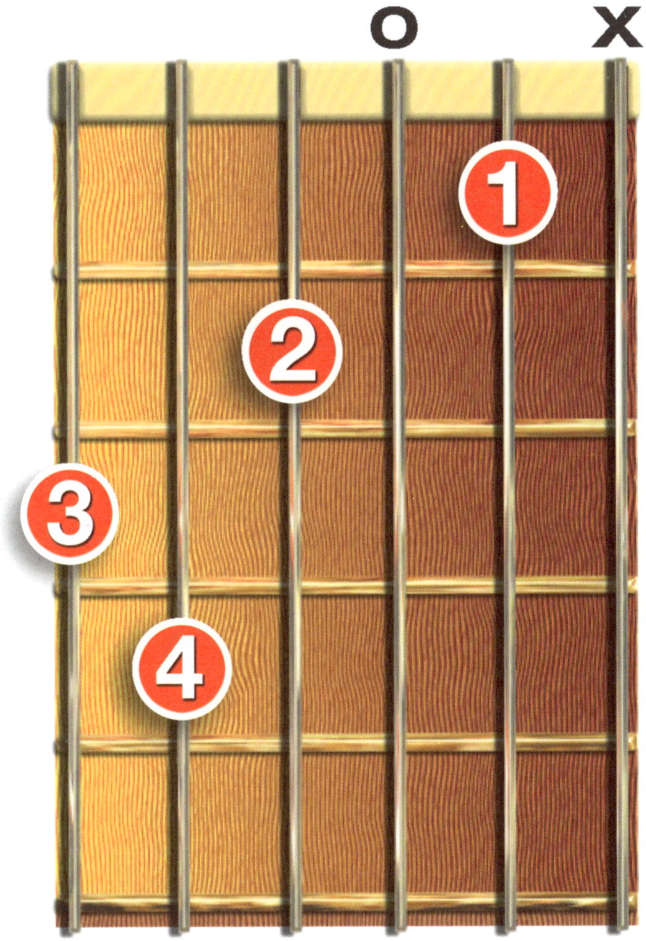

Bass String

Chord Spelling

1st (B♭), 3rd (D), 5th (F), 7th (A), 9th (C), 11th (E♭), 13th (G)

FREE ACCESS on smartphones including iPhone & Android

Using any QR code app scan and **HEAR** the chord

A
A♯/B♭
B
C
C♯/D♭
D
D♯/E♭
E
F
F♯/G♭
G
G♯/A♭

B
Major

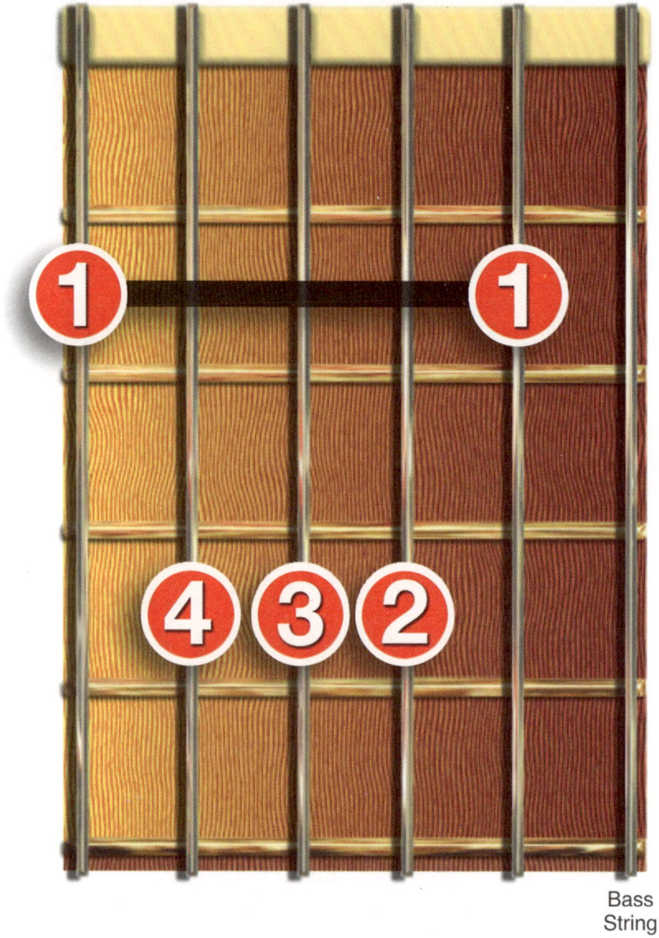

Chord Spelling

1st (B), 3rd (D♯), 5th (F♯)

FREE ACCESS on smartphones including iPhone & Android

Using any QR code app scan and **HEAR** the chord

Bm

Minor

Chord Spelling

1st (B), ♭3rd (D), 5th (F♯)

A
A♯/B♭
B
C
C♯/D♭
D
D♯/E♭
E
F
F♯/G♭
G
G♯/A♭

B+

Augmented Triad

Chord Spelling

1st (B), 3rd (D♯), ♯5th (Fx)

FREE ACCESS on smartphones including iPhone & Android

Using any QR code app scan and **HEAR** the chord

B°
Diminished Triad

Chord Spelling

1st (B), ♭3rd (D), ♭5th (F)

FREE ACCESS on smartphones including iPhone & Android

Using any QR code app scan and **HEAR** the chord

Bsus2

Suspended 2nd

Chord Spelling

1st (B), 2nd (C♯), 5th (F♯)

FREE ACCESS on smartphones including iPhone & Android

Using any QR code app scan and **HEAR** the chord

Bsus4

Suspended 4th

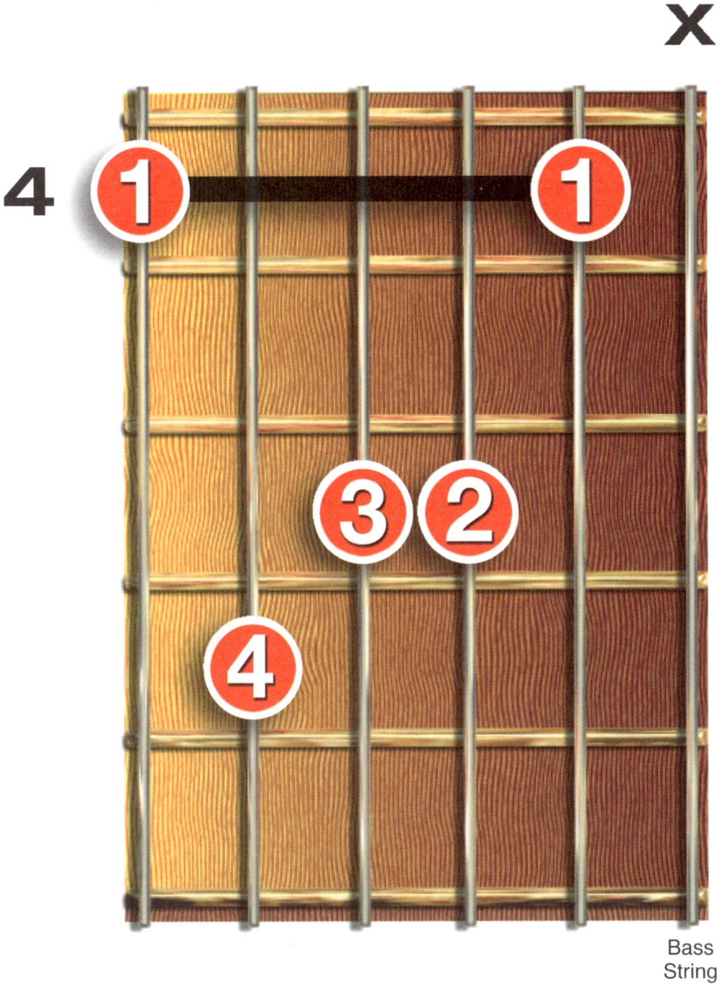

Chord Spelling

1st (B), 4th (E), 5th (F♯)

FREE ACCESS on smartphones including iPhone & Android

Using any QR code app scan and **HEAR** the chord

B5

5th (Power Chord)

Chord Spelling

1st (B), 5th (F♯)

FREE ACCESS on smartphones including iPhone & Android

Using any QR code app scan and **HEAR** the chord

B6
Major 6th

Chord Spelling

1st (B), 3rd (D♯), 5th (F♯), 6th (G♯)

FREE ACCESS on smartphones including iPhone & Android

Using any QR code app scan and **HEAR** the chord

A
A♯/B♭
B
C
C♯/D♭
D
D♯/E♭
E
F
F♯/G♭
G
G♯/A♭

Bm6

Minor 6th

Chord Spelling

1st (B), ♭3rd (D), 5th (F♯), 6th (G♯)

FREE ACCESS on smartphones including iPhone & Android

Using any QR code app scan and **HEAR** the chord

B6sus4

6th Suspended 4th

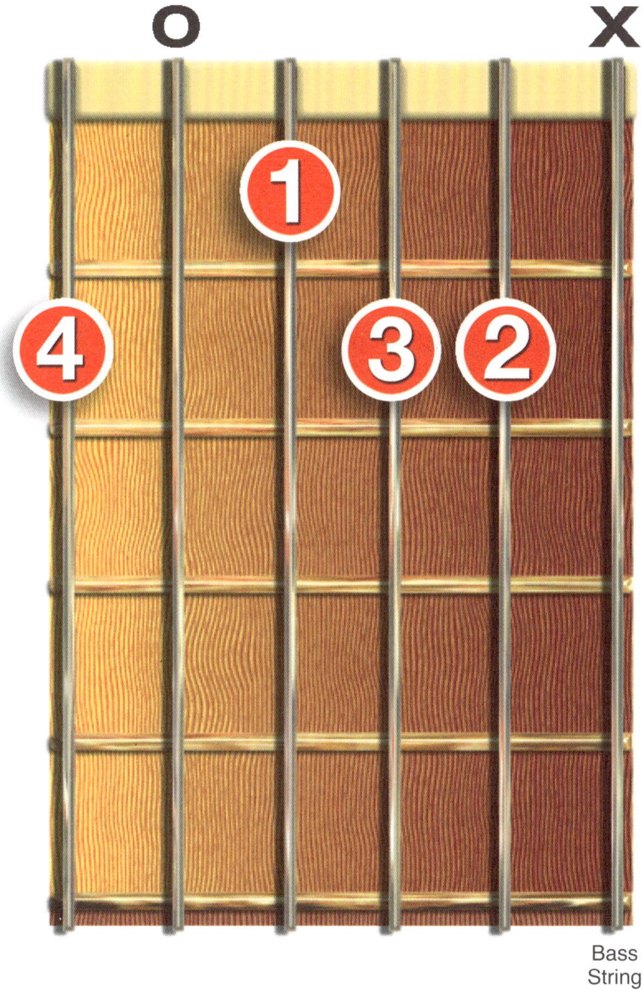

Chord Spelling

1st (B), 4th (E), 5th (F♯), 6th (G♯)

FREE ACCESS on smartphones including iPhone & Android

Using any QR code app scan and **HEAR** the chord

Bmaj7

Major 7th

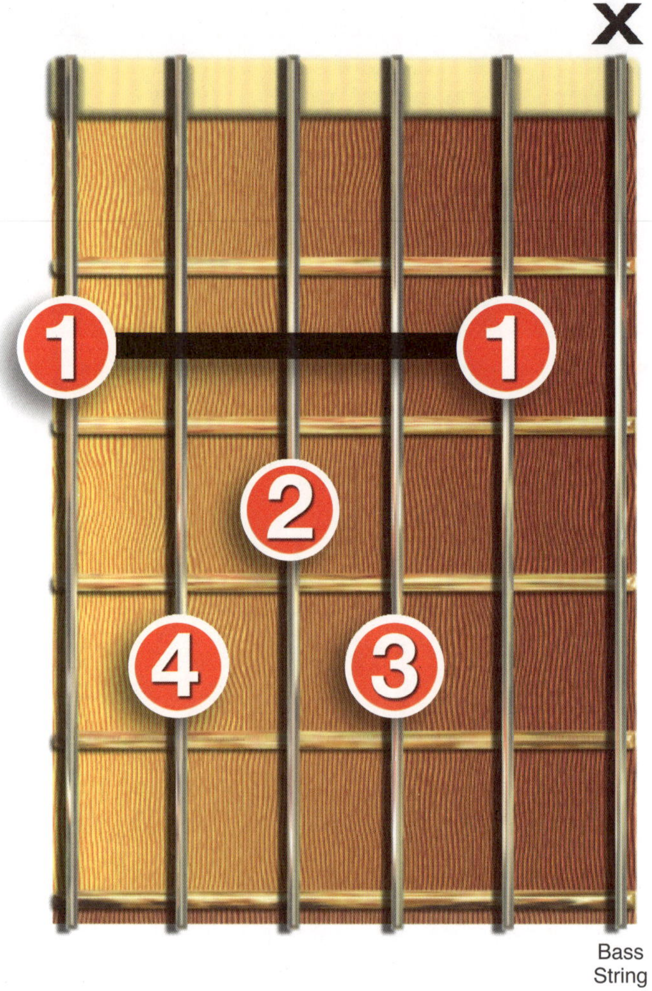

Chord Spelling

1st (B), 3rd (D♯), 5th (F♯), 7th (A♯)

Bm7

Minor 7th

Chord Spelling

1st (B), ♭3rd (D), 5th (F♯), ♭7th (A)

FREE ACCESS on smartphones including iPhone & Android

Using any QR code app scan and **HEAR** the chord

A
A♯/B♭
B
C
C♯/D♭
D
D♯/E♭
E
F
F♯/G♭
G
G♯/A♭

B7

Dominant 7th

Chord Spelling

1st (B), 3rd (D♯), 5th (F♯), ♭7th (A)

FREE ACCESS on smartphones including iPhone & Android

Using any QR code app scan and **HEAR** the chord

B°7
Diminished 7th

Chord Spelling

1st (B), ♭3rd (D), ♭5th (F), ♭♭7th (A♭)

FREE ACCESS on smartphones including iPhone & Android

Using any QR code app scan and **HEAR** the chord

A
A♯/B♭
B
C
C♯/D♭
D
D♯/E♭
E
F
F♯/G♭
G
G♯/A♭

B7sus4

Dominant 7th Suspended 4th

O
X
4
3
2
1
Bass
String

Chord Spelling

1st (B), 4th (E), 5th (F♯), ♭7th (A)

FREE ACCESS on smartphones including iPhone & Android

Using any QR code app scan and **HEAR** the chord

Bmaj9
Major 9th

Chord Spelling

1st (B), 3rd (D♯), 5th (F♯), 7th (A♯), 9th (C♯)

FREE ACCESS on smartphones including iPhone & Android

Using any QR code app scan and **HEAR** the chord

Bm9

Minor 9th

Chord Spelling

1st (B), ♭3rd (D), 5th (F♯), ♭7th (A), 9th (C♯)

B9

Dominant 9th

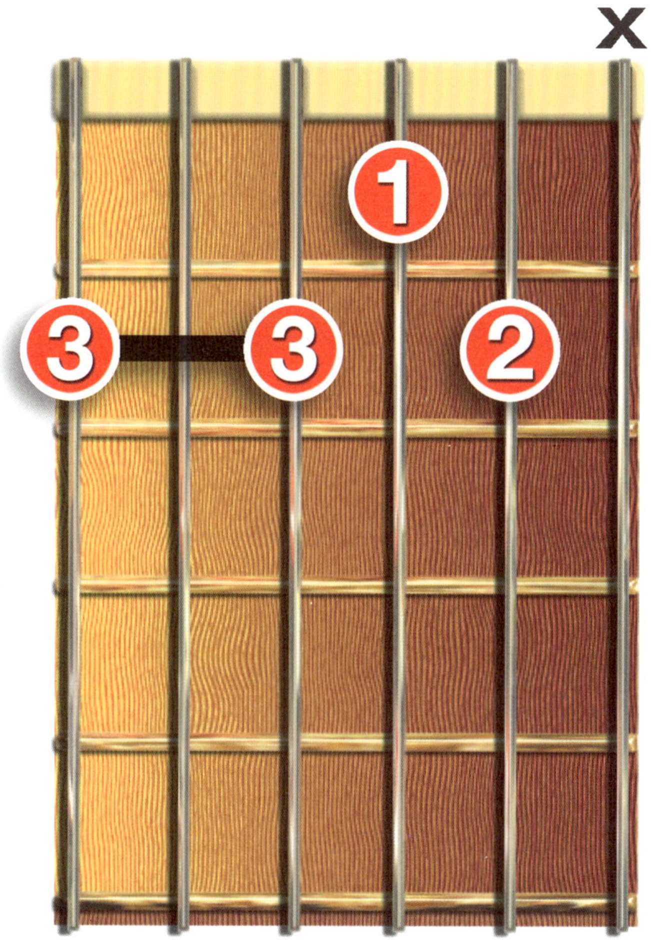

Bass String

Chord Spelling

1st (B), 3rd (D♯), 5th (F♯), ♭7th (A), 9th (C♯)

FREE ACCESS on smartphones including iPhone & Android

Using any QR code app scan and **HEAR** the chord

A
A♯/B♭
B
C
C♯/D♭
D
D♯/E♭
E
F
F♯/G♭
G
G♯/A♭

Bmaj11

Major 11th

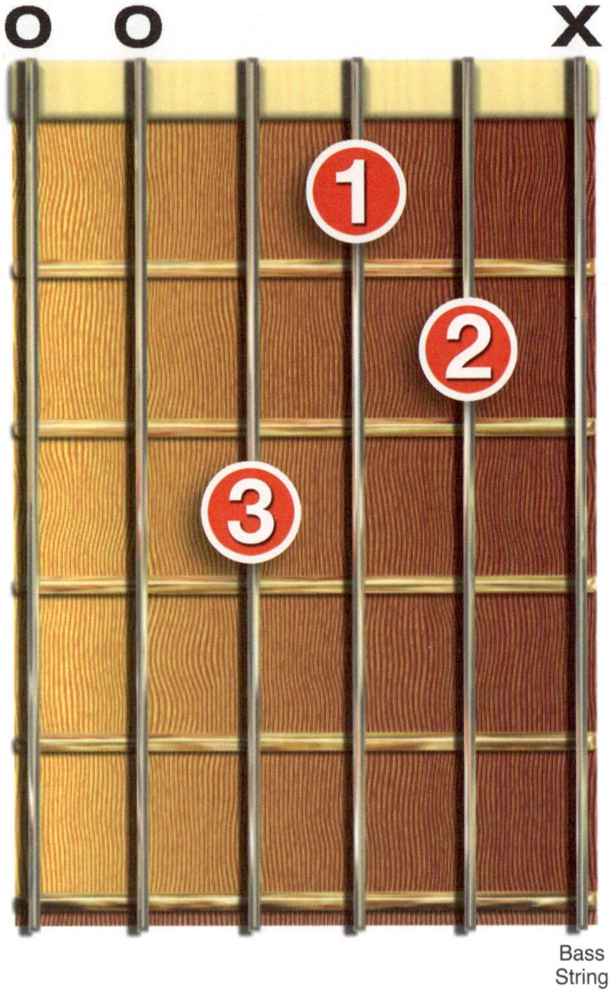

Chord Spelling

1st (B), 3rd (D♯), 5th (F♯), 7th (A♯), 9th (C♯), 11th (E)

FREE ACCESS on smartphones including iPhone & Android

Using any QR code app scan and **HEAR** the chord

Bmaj13

Major 13th

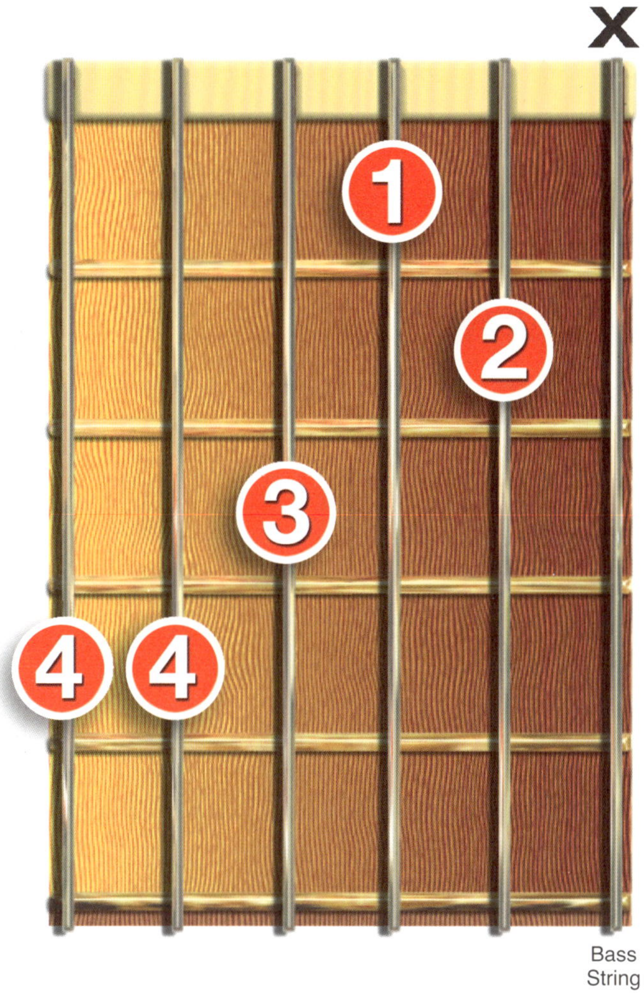

Chord Spelling

1st (B), 3rd (D♯), 5th (F♯), 7th (A♯), 9th (C♯), 11th (E), 13th (G♯)

FREE ACCESS on smartphones including iPhone & Android

Using any QR code app scan and **HEAR** the chord

C

Major

Chord Spelling

1st (C), 3rd (E), 5th (G)

FREE ACCESS on smartphones including iPhone & Android

Using any QR code app scan and **HEAR** the chord

Cm

Minor

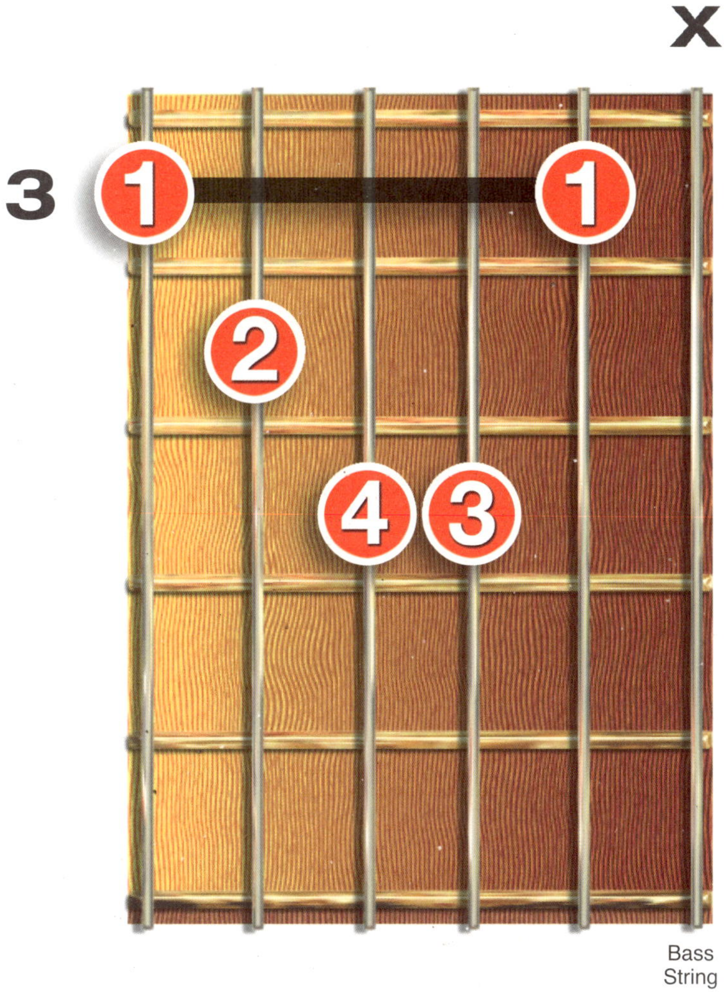
x
3
1
1
2
4
3
Bass String

Chord Spelling

1st (C), ♭3rd (E♭), 5th (G)

FREE ACCESS on smartphones including iPhone & Android

Using any QR code app scan and **HEAR** the chord

C+

Augmented Triad

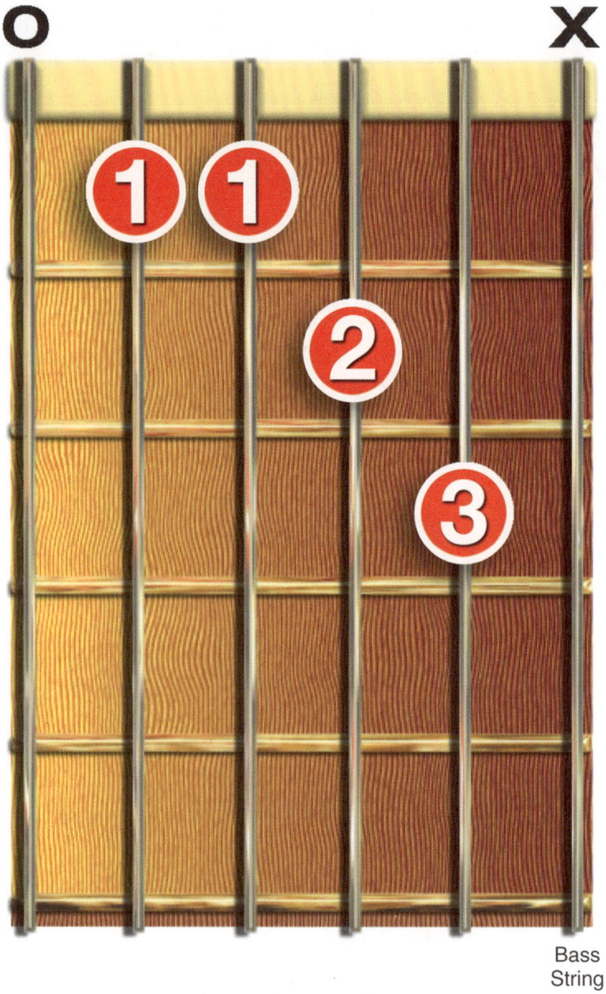

Chord Spelling

1st (C), 3rd (E), ♯5th (G♯)

FREE ACCESS on smartphones including iPhone & Android

Using any QR code app scan and **HEAR** the chord

C°

Diminished Triad

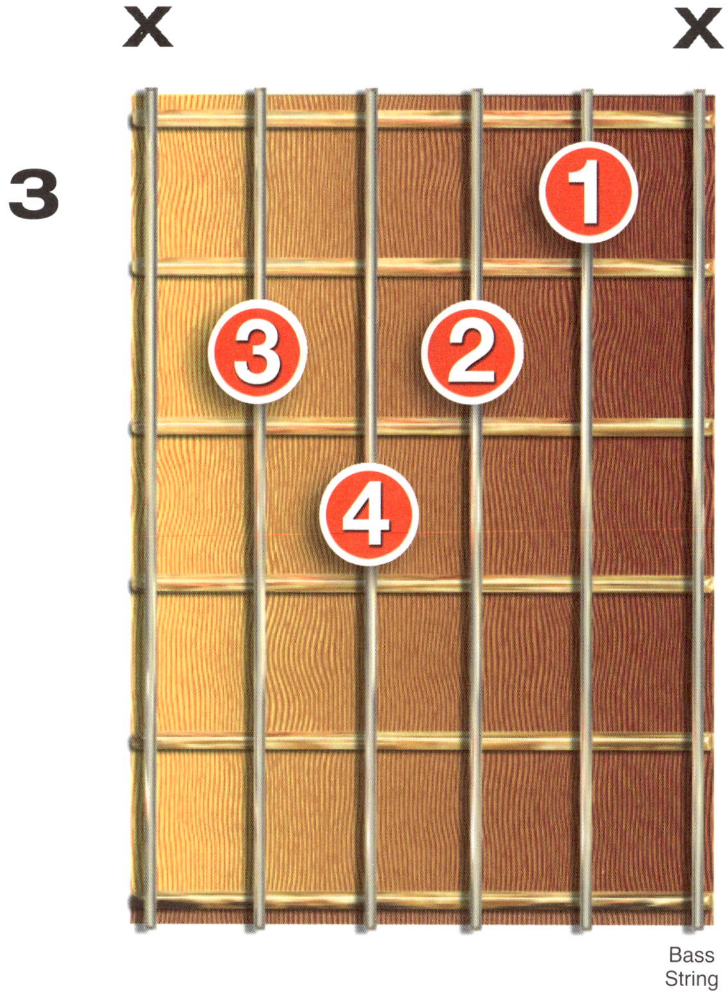

Chord Spelling

1st (C), ♭3rd (E♭), ♭5th (G♭)

FREE ACCESS on smartphones including iPhone & Android

Using any QR code app scan and **HEAR** the chord

Csus2

Suspended 2nd

O O X
3 2 1
Bass
String

Chord Spelling

1st (C), 2nd (D), 5th (G)

FREE ACCESS on smartphones including iPhone & Android

Using any QR code app scan and **HEAR** the chord

Csus4

Suspended 4th

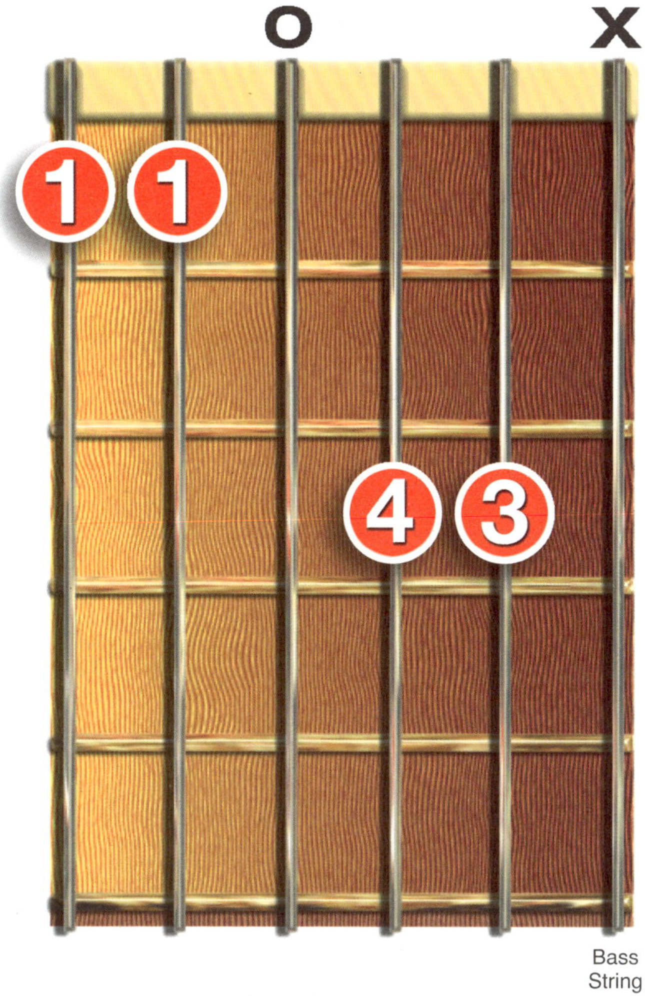
o
x
1
1
4
3
Bass String

Chord Spelling

1st (C), 4th (F), 5th (G)

FREE ACCESS on smartphones including iPhone & Android

Using any QR code app scan and **HEAR** the chord

C5

5th (Power Chord)

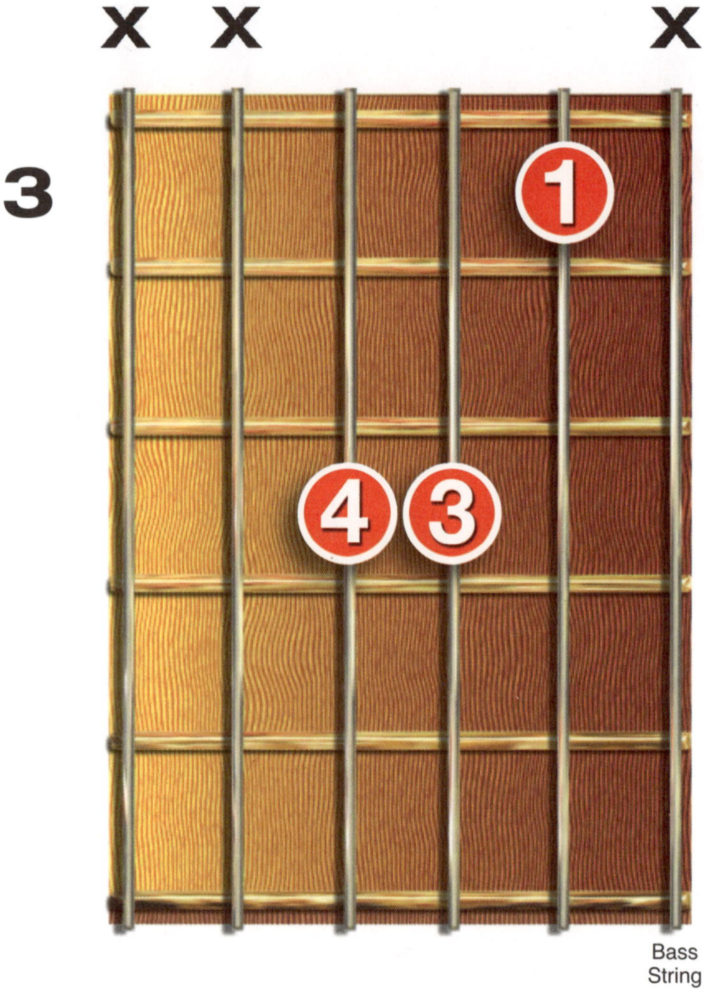
X X X
3
1
4 3
Bass String

Chord Spelling

1st (C), 5th (G)

FREE ACCESS on smartphones including iPhone & Android

Using any QR code app scan and **HEAR** the chord

C6

Major 6th

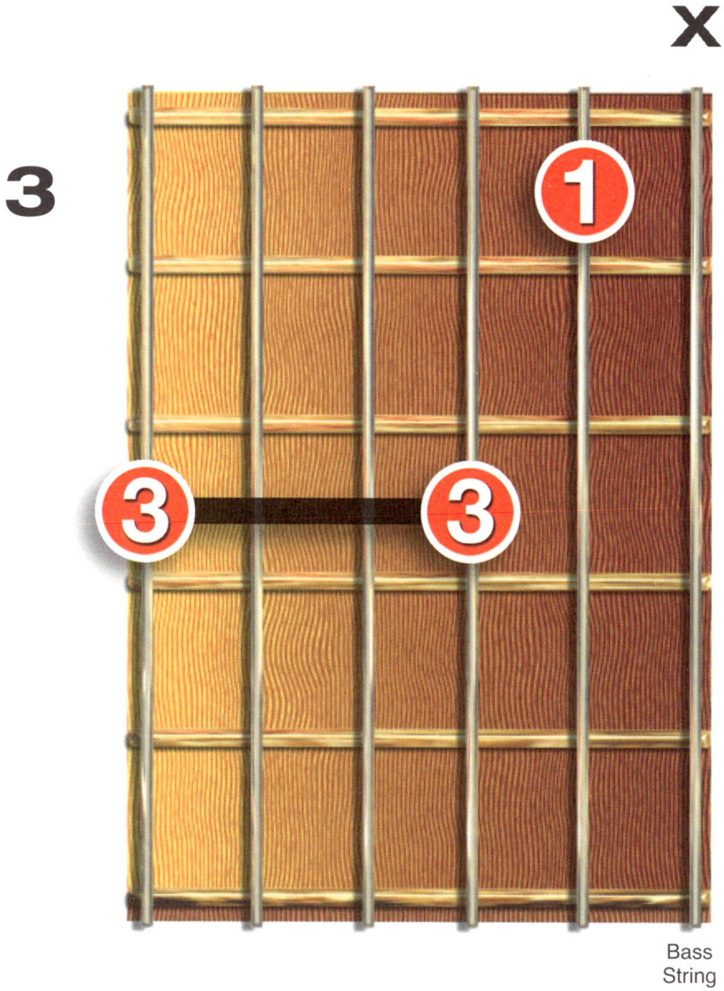
x
3
1
3
3
Bass
String

Chord Spelling

1st (C), 3rd (E), 5th (G), 6th (A)

FREE ACCESS on smartphones including iPhone & Android

Using any QR code app scan and **HEAR** the chord

Cm6

Minor 6th

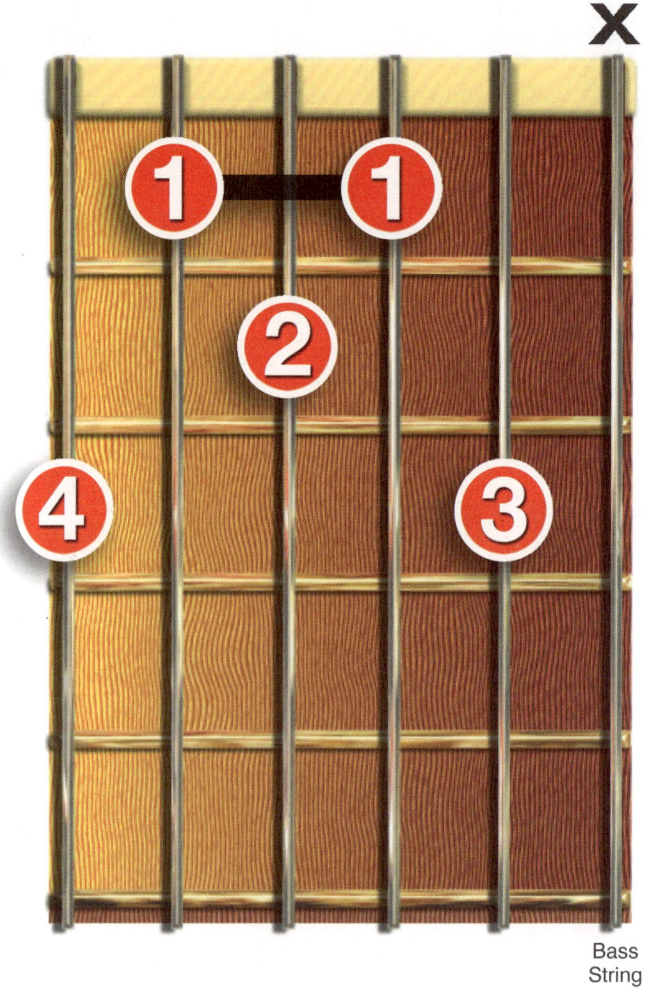

Chord Spelling

1st (C), ♭3rd (E♭), 5th (G), 6th (A)

C6sus4

6th Suspended 4th

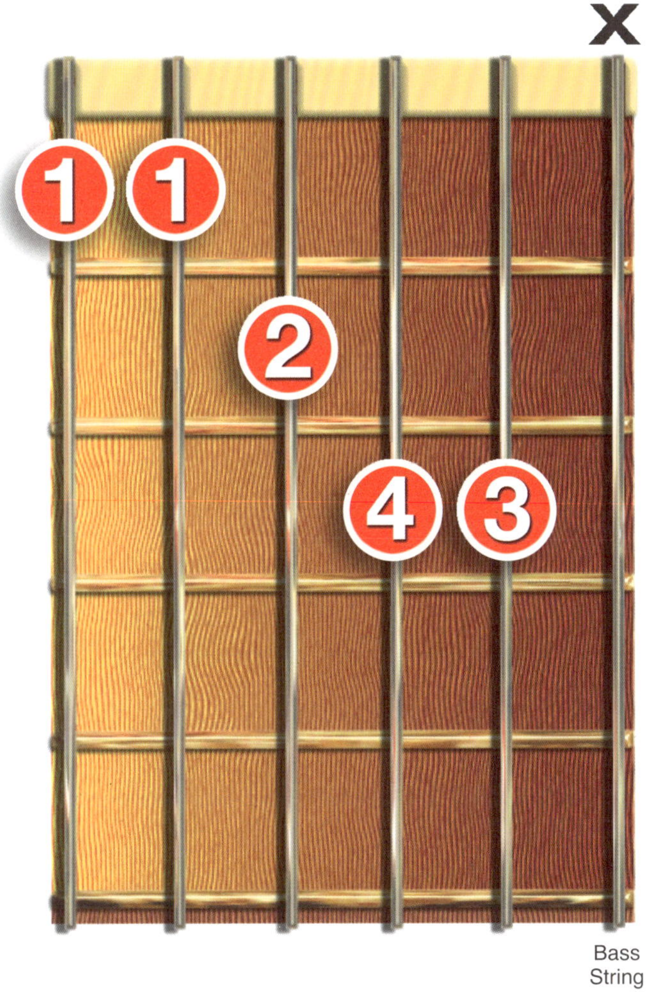

Chord Spelling

1st (C), 4th (F), 5th (G), 6th (A)

FREE ACCESS on smartphones including iPhone & Android

Using any QR code app scan and **HEAR** the chord

A
A#/B♭
B
C
C#/D♭
D
D#/E♭
E
F
F#/G♭
G
G#/A♭

Cmaj7

Major 7th

Chord Spelling

1st (C), 3rd (E), 5th (G), 7th (B)

FREE ACCESS on smartphones including iPhone & Android

Using any QR code app scan and **HEAR** the chord

Cm7

Minor 7th

Chord Spelling

1st (C), ♭3rd (E♭), 5th (G), ♭7th (B♭)

FREE ACCESS on smartphones including iPhone & Android

Using any QR code app scan and **HEAR** the chord

C7

Dominant 7th

Chord Spelling

1st (C), 3rd (E), 5th (G), ♭7th (B♭)

FREE ACCESS on smartphones including iPhone & Android

Using any QR code app scan and **HEAR** the chord

C°7

Diminished 7th

Chord Spelling

1st (C), ♭3rd (E♭), ♭5th (G♭), ♭♭7th (B♭♭)

FREE ACCESS on smartphones including iPhone & Android

Using any QR code app scan and **HEAR** the chord

C7sus4

Dominant 7th Suspended 4th

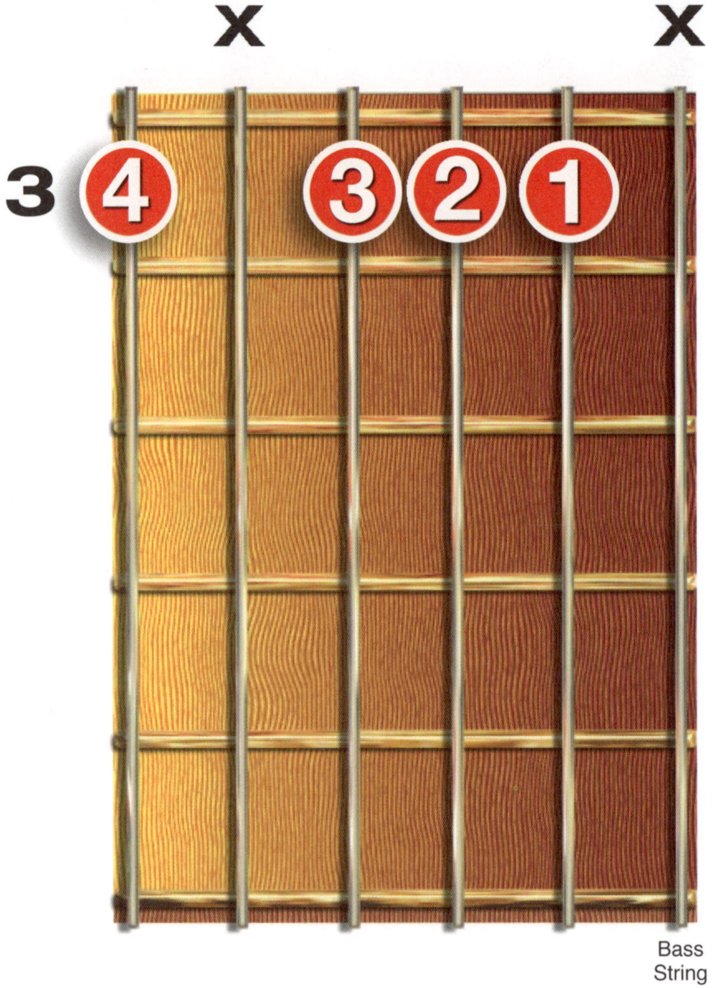
X
X
3
4
3
2
1
Bass String

Chord Spelling

1st (C), 4th (F), 5th (G), ♭7th (B♭)

FREE ACCESS on smartphones including iPhone & Android

Using any QR code app scan and **HEAR** the chord

Cmaj9

Major 9th

Chord Spelling

1st (C), 3rd (E), 5th (G), 7th (B), 9th (D)

Cm9

Minor 9th

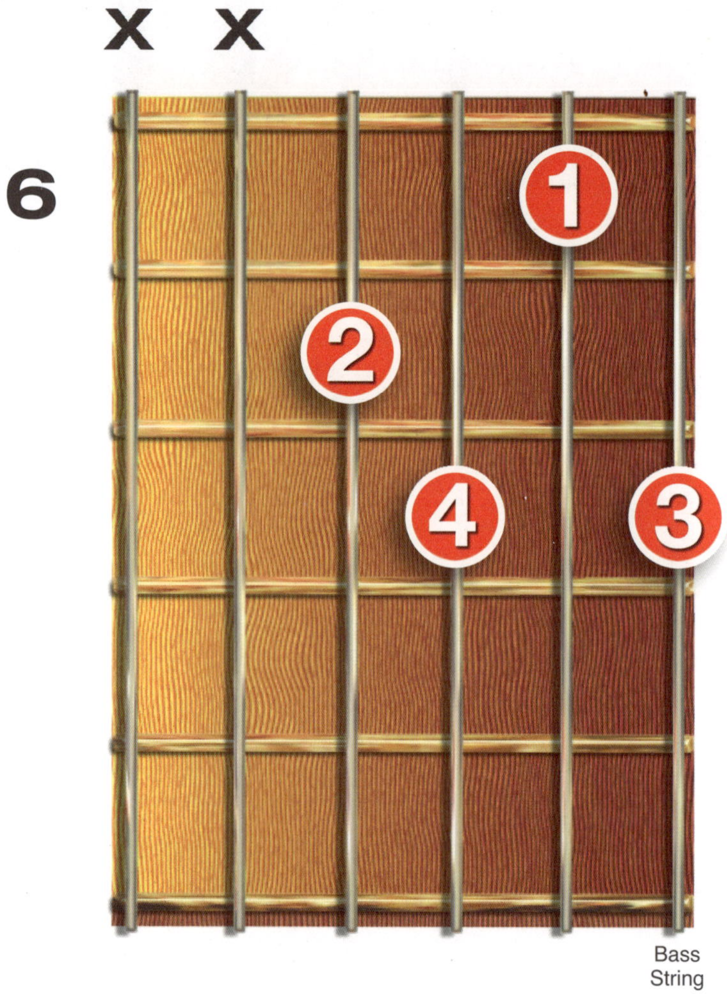
X X
6
1
2
4
3
Bass String

Chord Spelling

1st (C), ♭3rd (E♭), 5th (G), ♭7th (B♭), 9th (D)

FREE ACCESS on smartphones including iPhone & Android

Using any QR code app scan and **HEAR** the chord

C9

Dominant 9th

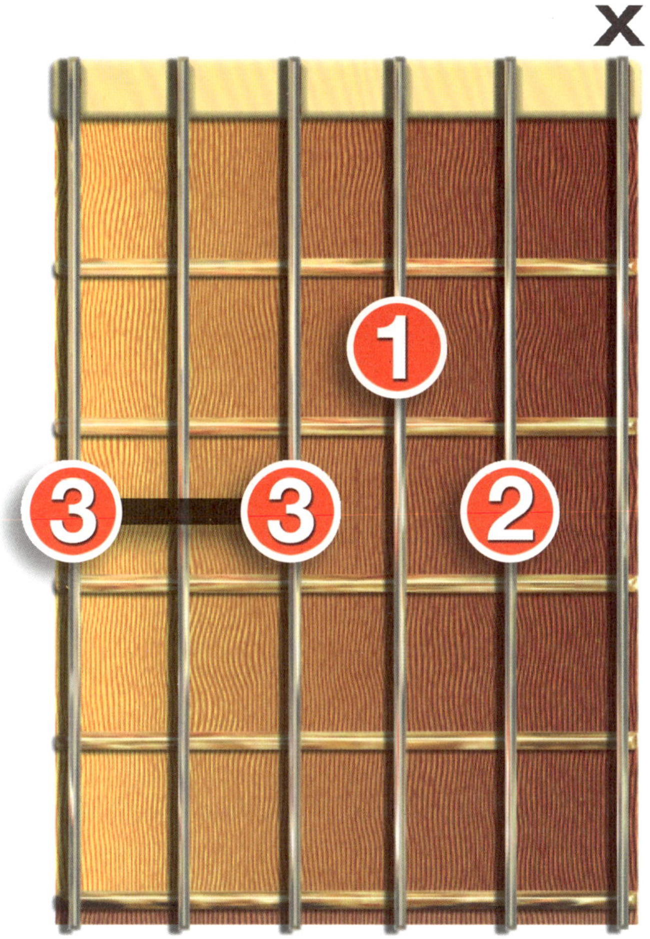

Chord Spelling

1st (C), 3rd (E), 5th (G), ♭7th (B♭), 9th (D)

FREE ACCESS on smartphones including iPhone & Android

Using any QR code app scan and **HEAR** the chord

Cmaj11

Major 11th

Chord Spelling

1st (C), 3rd (E), 5th (G), 7th (B), 9th (D), 11th (F)

Cmaj13
Major 13th

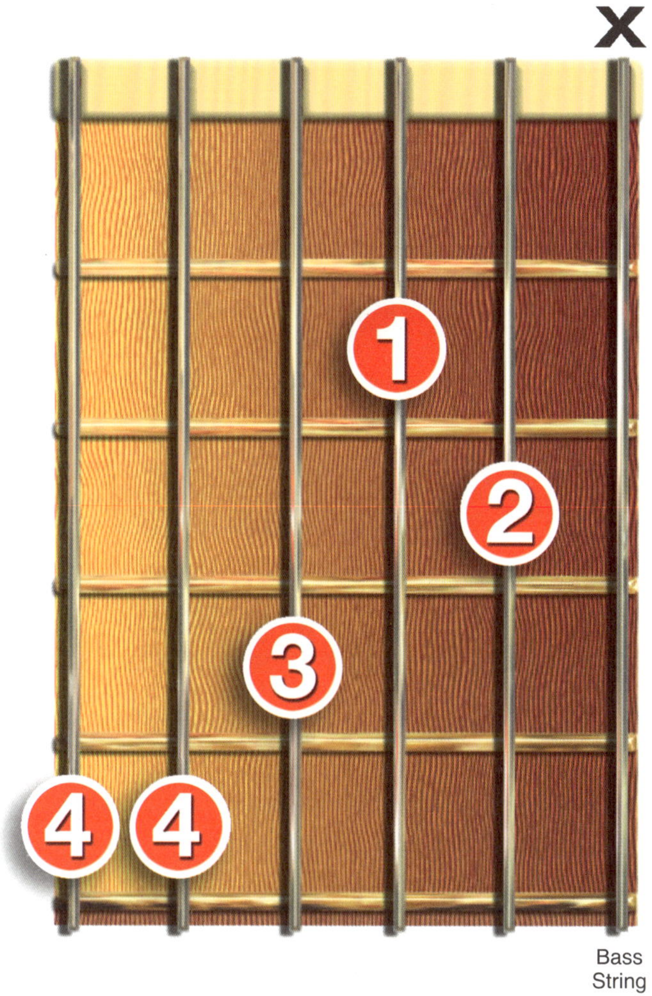

Chord Spelling

1st (C), 3rd (E), 5th (G), 7th (B), 9th (D), 11th (F), 13th (A)

FREE ACCESS on smartphones including iPhone & Android

Using any QR code app scan and **HEAR** the chord

C♯/D♭
Major

Chord Spelling

1st (C♯), 3rd (E♯), 5th (G♯)

FREE ACCESS on smartphones including iPhone & Android

Using any QR code app scan and **HEAR** the chord

C♯/D♭m

Minor

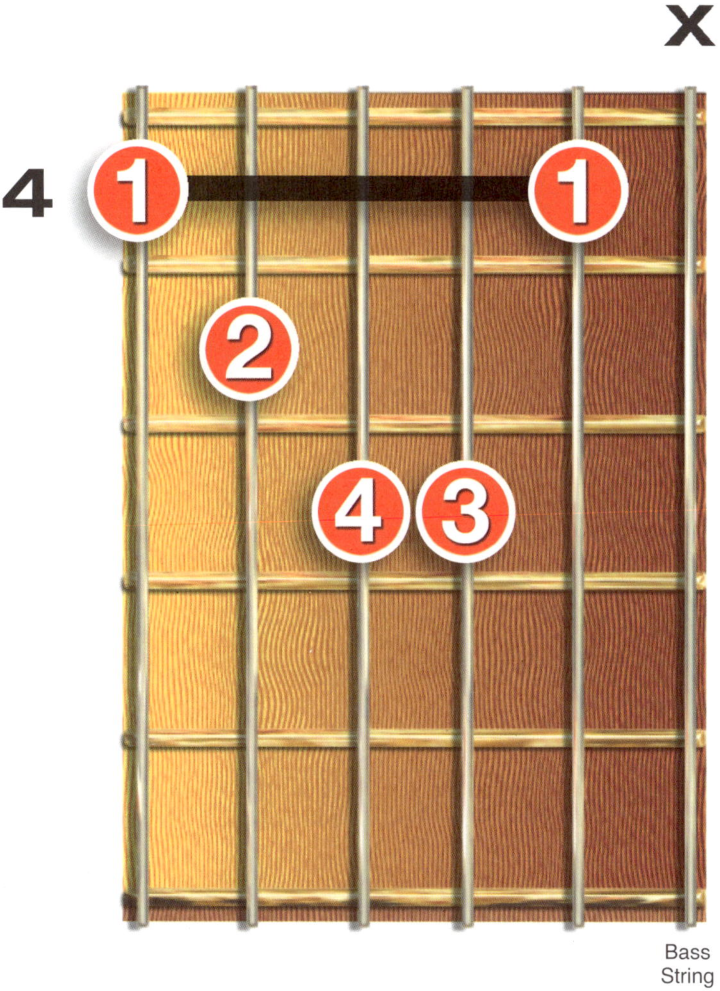

Chord Spelling

1st (C♯), ♭3rd (E), 5th (G♯)

FREE ACCESS on smartphones including iPhone & Android

Using any QR code app scan and **HEAR** the chord

C♯/D♭+
Augmented Triad

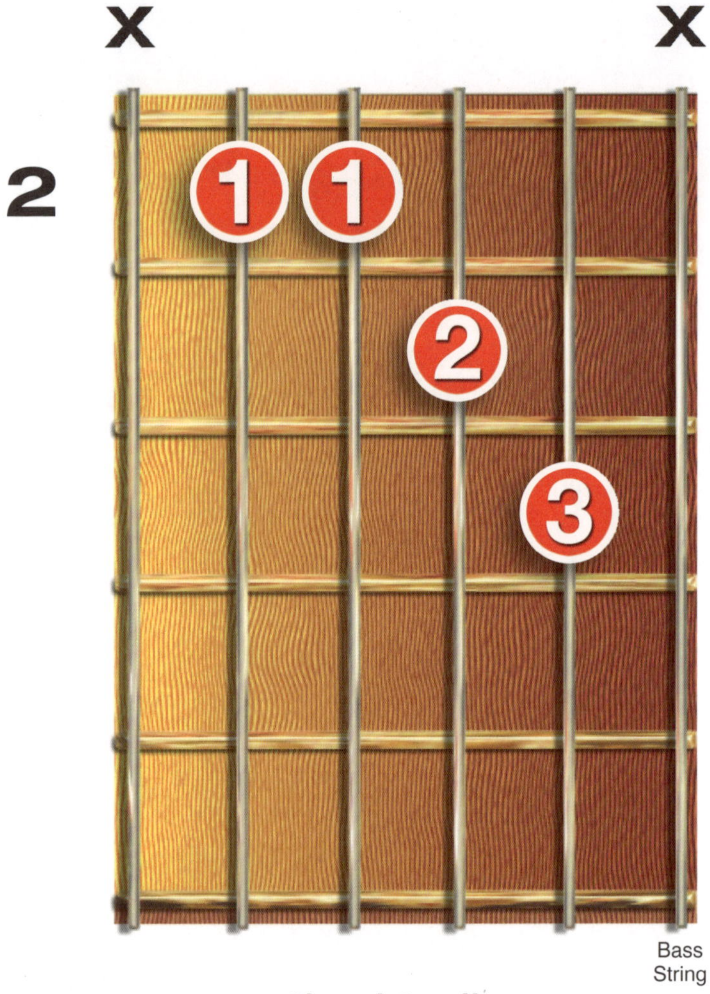

Chord Spelling

1st (C♯), 3rd (E♯), ♯5th (Gx)

FREE ACCESS on smartphones including iPhone & Android

Using any QR code app scan and **HEAR** the chord

C♯/D♭°

Diminished Triad

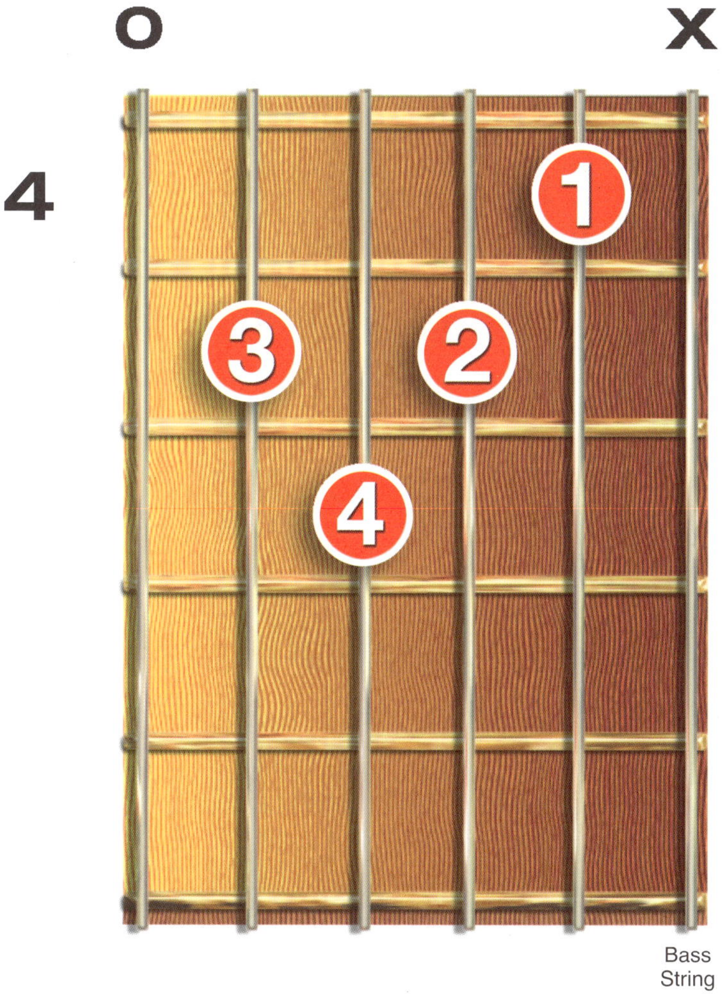

Chord Spelling

1st (C♯), ♭3rd (E), ♭5th (G)

FREE ACCESS on smartphones including iPhone & Android

Using any QR code app scan and **HEAR** the chord

C♯/D♭sus2

Suspended 2nd

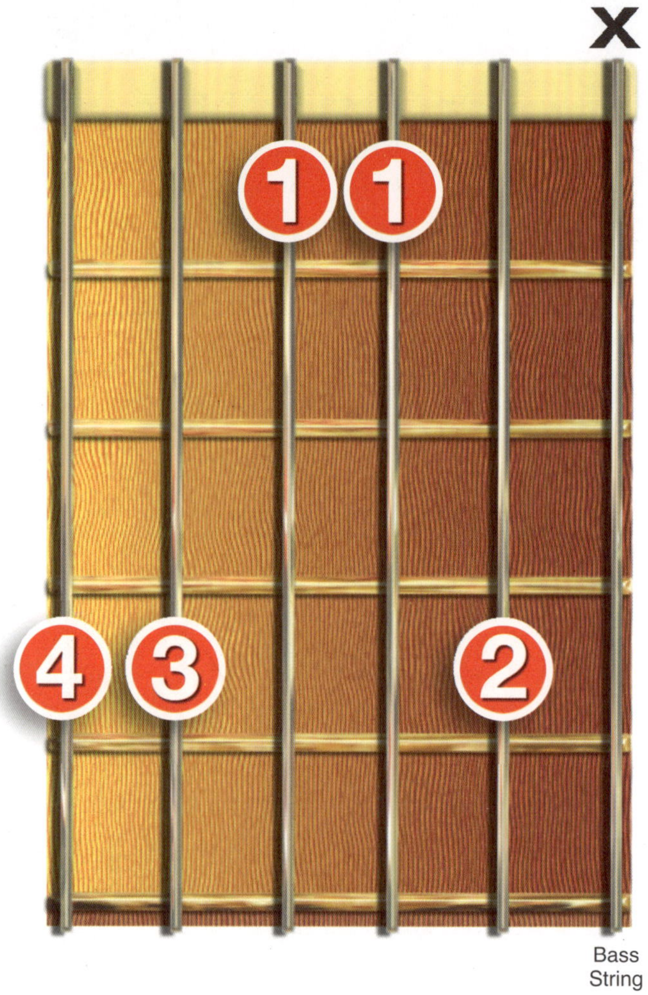

Chord Spelling

1st (C♯), 2nd (D♯), 5th (G♯)

FREE ACCESS on smartphones including iPhone & Android

Using any QR code app scan and **HEAR** the chord

C♯/D♭sus4

Suspended 4th

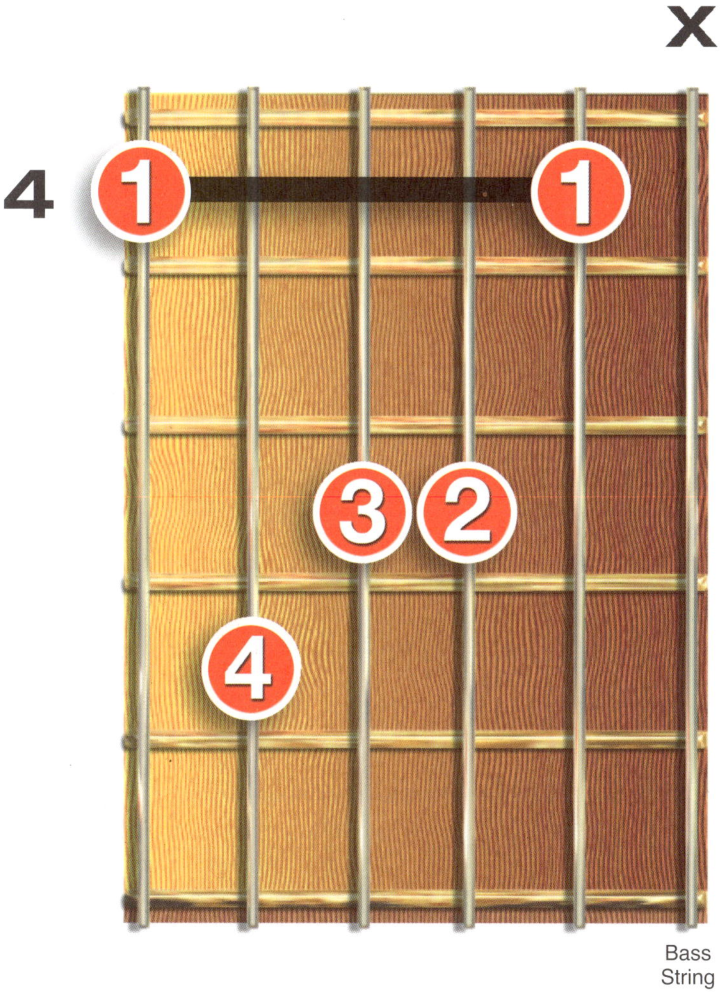
x
4
1
1
3
2
4
Bass String

Chord Spelling

1st (C♯), 4th (F♯), 5th (G♯)

FREE ACCESS on smartphones including iPhone & Android

Using any QR code app scan and **HEAR** the chord

C♯/D♭5

5th (Power Chord)

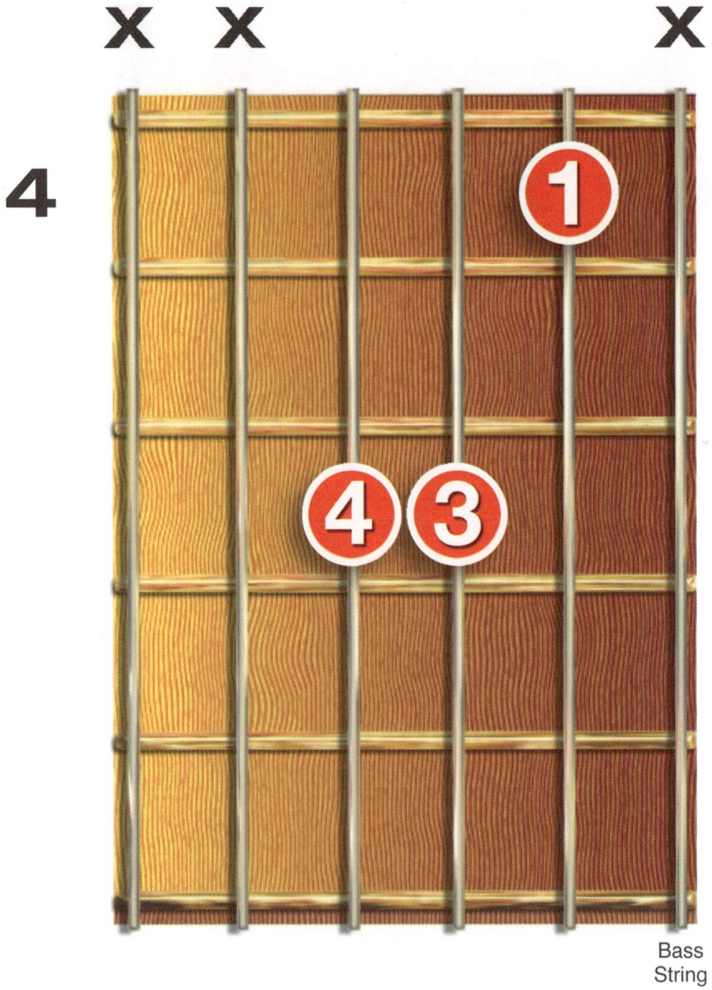
X X X
4
1
4 3
Bass String

Chord Spelling

1st (C♯), 5th (G♯)

FREE ACCESS on smartphones including iPhone & Android

Using any QR code app scan and **HEAR** the chord

C♯/D♭6
Major 6th

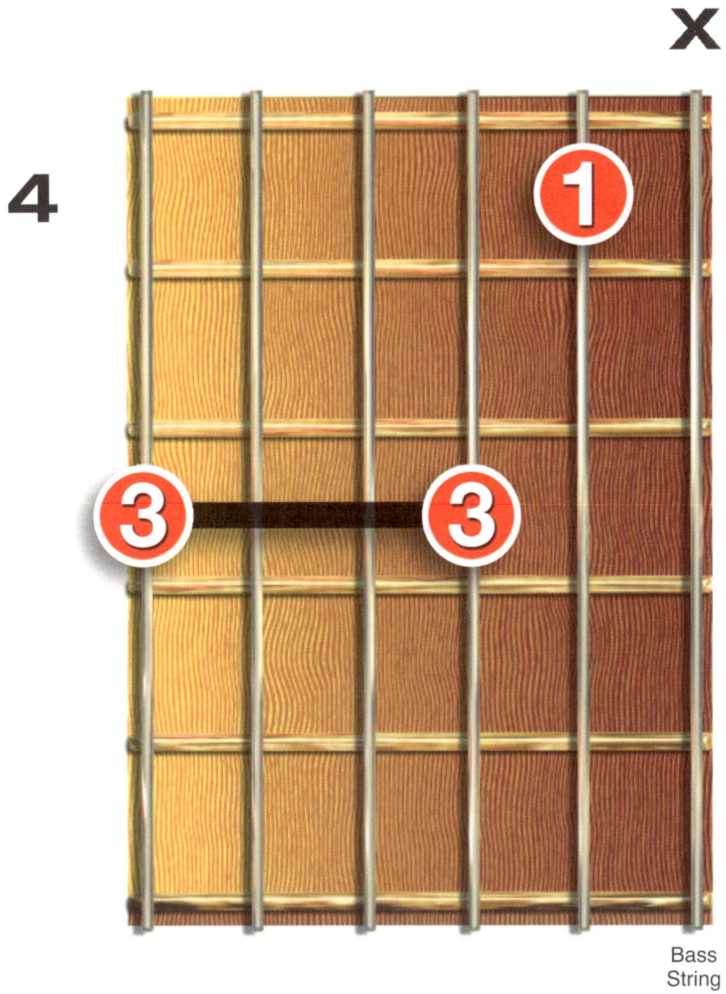

Chord Spelling

1st (C♯), 3rd (E♯), 5th (G♯), 6th (A♯)

FREE ACCESS on smartphones including iPhone & Android

Using any QR code app scan and **HEAR** the chord

C♯/D♭m6

Minor 6th

Chord Spelling

1st (C♯), ♭3rd (E), 5th (G♯), 6th (A♯)

FREE ACCESS on smartphones including iPhone & Android

Using any QR code app scan and **HEAR** the chord

C♯/D♭6sus4

6th Suspended 4th

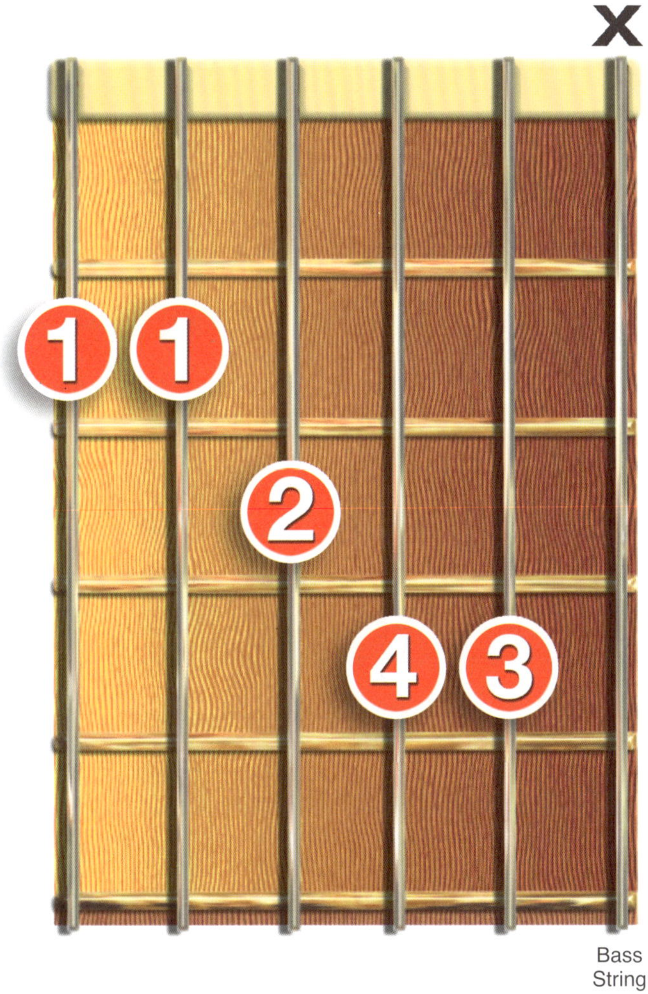

Chord Spelling

1st (C♯), 4th (F♯), 5th (G♯), 6th (A♯)

FREE ACCESS on smartphones including iPhone & Android

Using any QR code app scan and **HEAR** the chord

C♯/D♭maj7

Major 7th

Chord Spelling

1st (C♯), 3rd (E♯), 5th (G♯), 7th (B♯)

FREE ACCESS on smartphones including iPhone & Android

Using any QR code app scan and **HEAR** the chord

C♯/D♭m7

Minor 7th

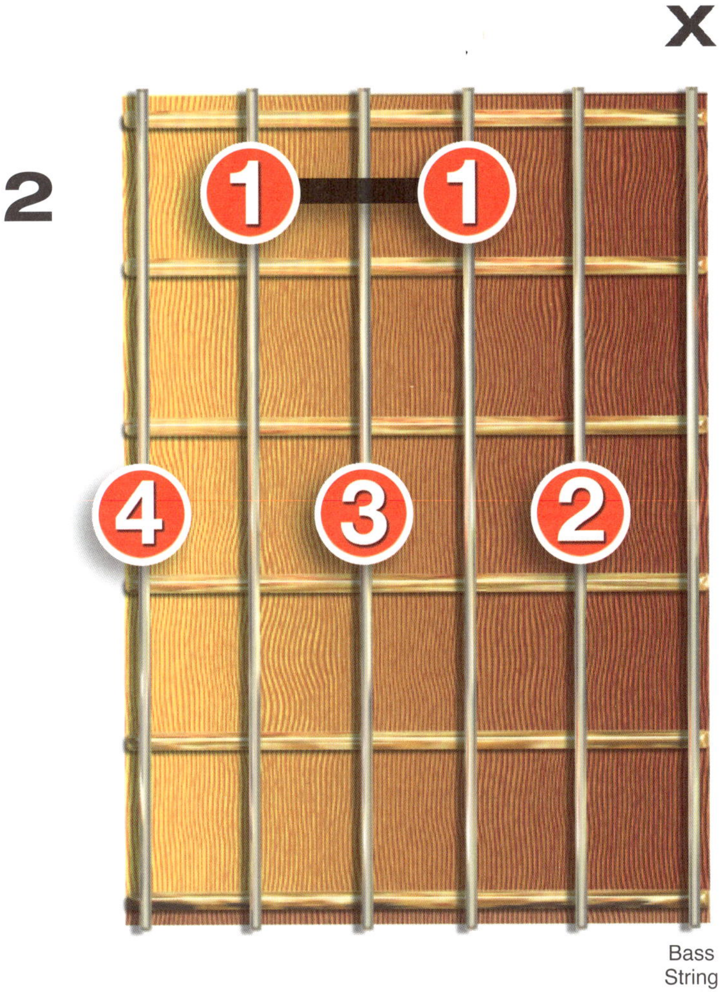

Chord Spelling

1st (C♯), ♭3rd (E), 5th (G♯), ♭7th (B)

FREE ACCESS on smartphones including iPhone & Android

Using any QR code app scan and **HEAR** the chord

C♯/D♭7
Dominant 7th

Chord Spelling

1st (C♯), 3rd (E♯), 5th (G♯), ♭7th (B)

FREE ACCESS on smartphones including iPhone & Android

Using any QR code app scan and **HEAR** the chord

C♯/D♭°7
Diminished 7th

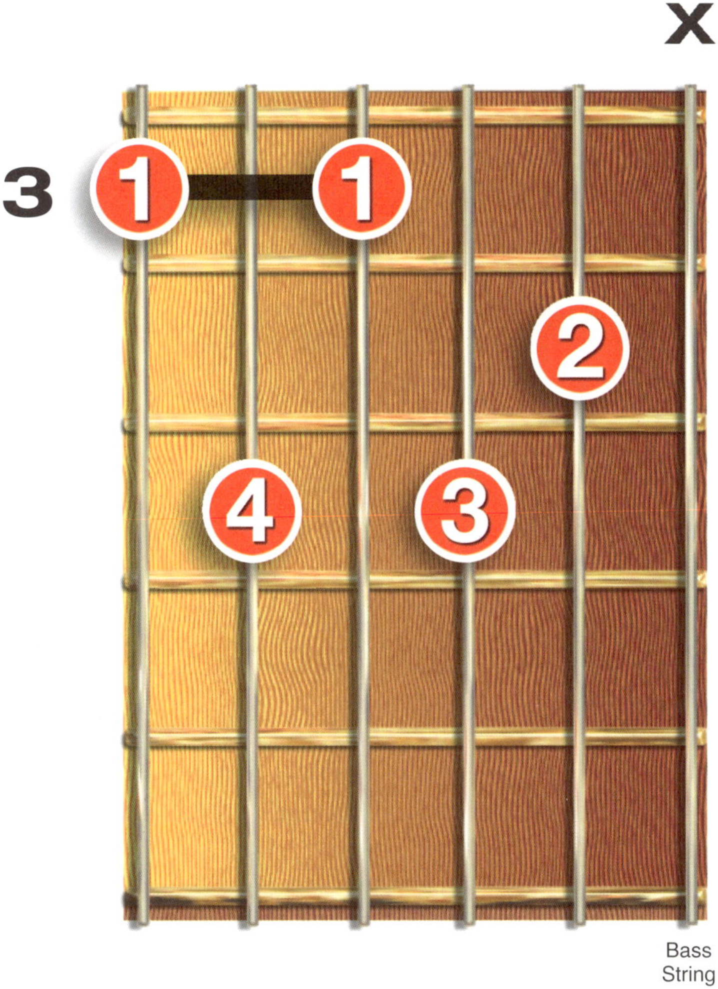

Chord Spelling

1st (C♯), ♭3rd (E), ♭5th (G), 𝄫7th (B♭)

FREE ACCESS on smartphones including iPhone & Android

Using any QR code app scan and **HEAR** the chord

C♯/D♭7sus4

Dominant 7th Suspended 4th

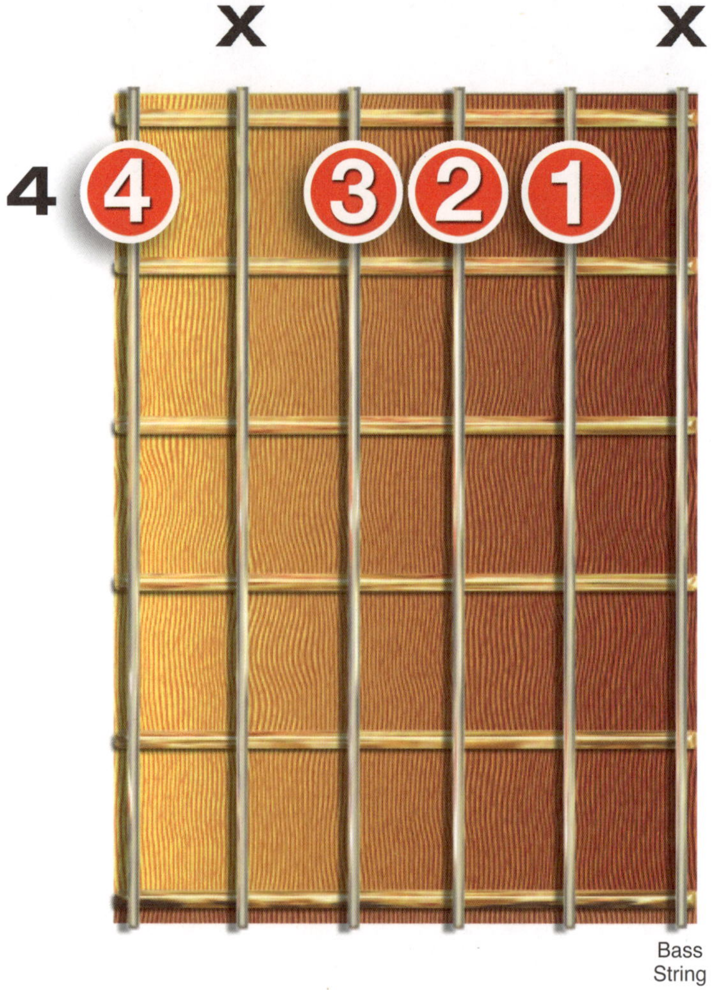

Chord Spelling

1st (C♯), 4th (F♯), 5th (G♯), ♭7th (B)

FREE ACCESS on smartphones including iPhone & Android

Using any QR code app scan and **HEAR** the chord

C♯/D♭maj9
Major 9th

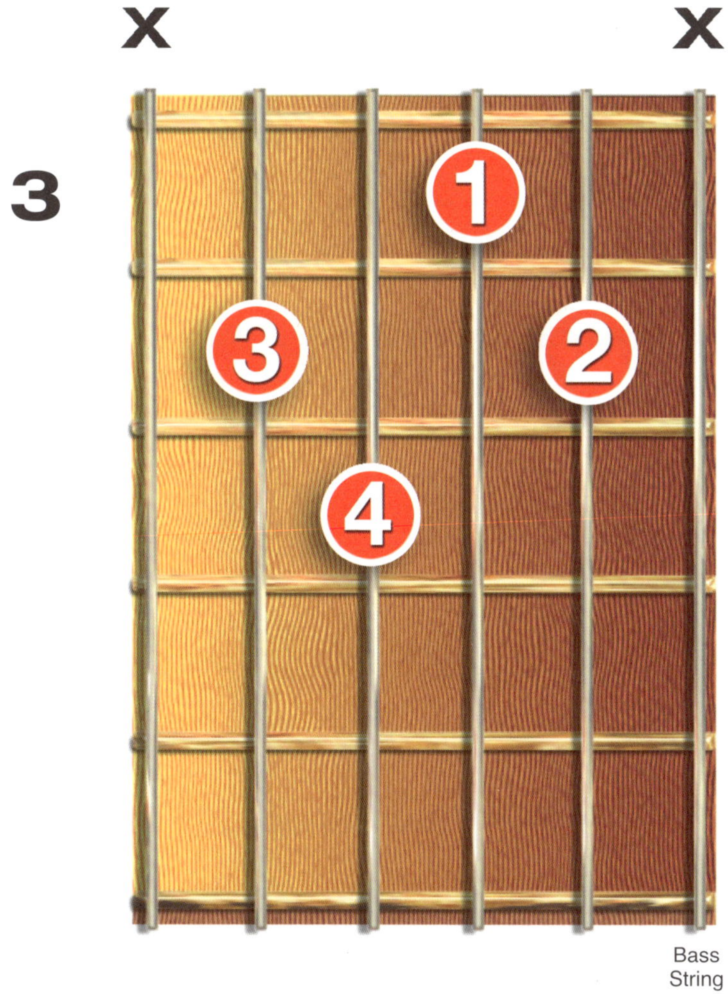

Chord Spelling

1st (C♯), 3rd (E♯), 5th (G♯), 7th (B♯), 9th (D♯)

FREE ACCESS on smartphones including iPhone & Android

Using any QR code app scan and **HEAR** the chord

C♯/D♭m9
Minor 9th

Chord Spelling

1st (C♯), ♭3rd (E), 5th (G♯), ♭7th (B), 9th (D♯)

FREE ACCESS on smartphones including iPhone & Android

Using any QR code app scan and **HEAR** the chord

C♯/D♭9

Dominant 9th

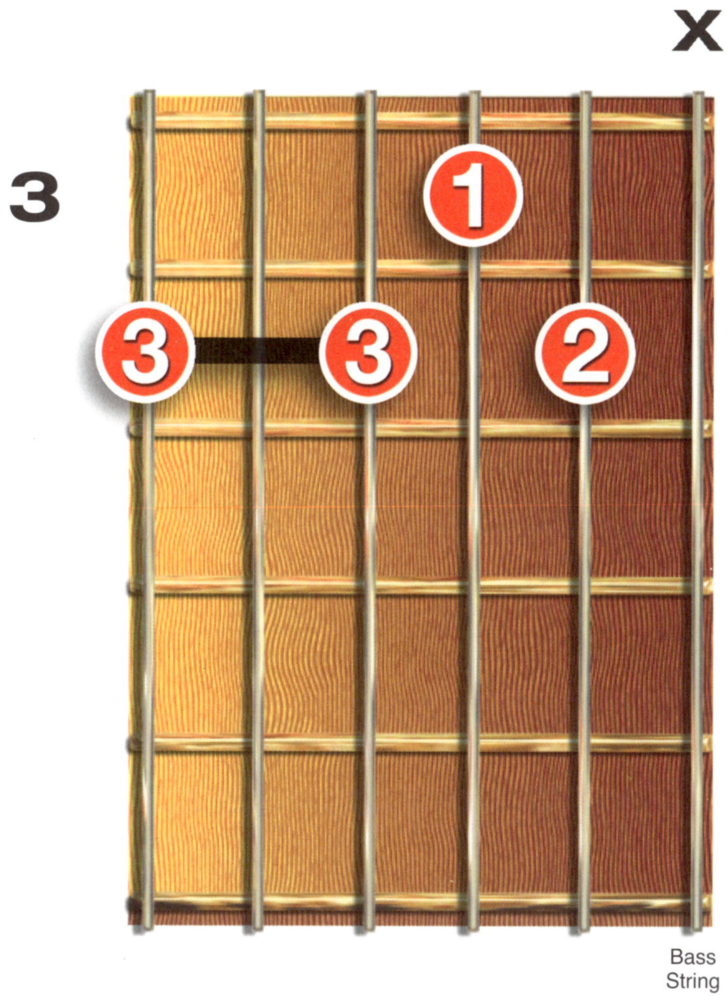

Chord Spelling

1st (C♯), 3rd (E♯), 5th (G♯), ♭7th (B), 9th (D♯)

FREE ACCESS on smartphones including iPhone & Android

Using any QR code app scan and **HEAR** the chord

C♯/D♭maj11

Major 11th

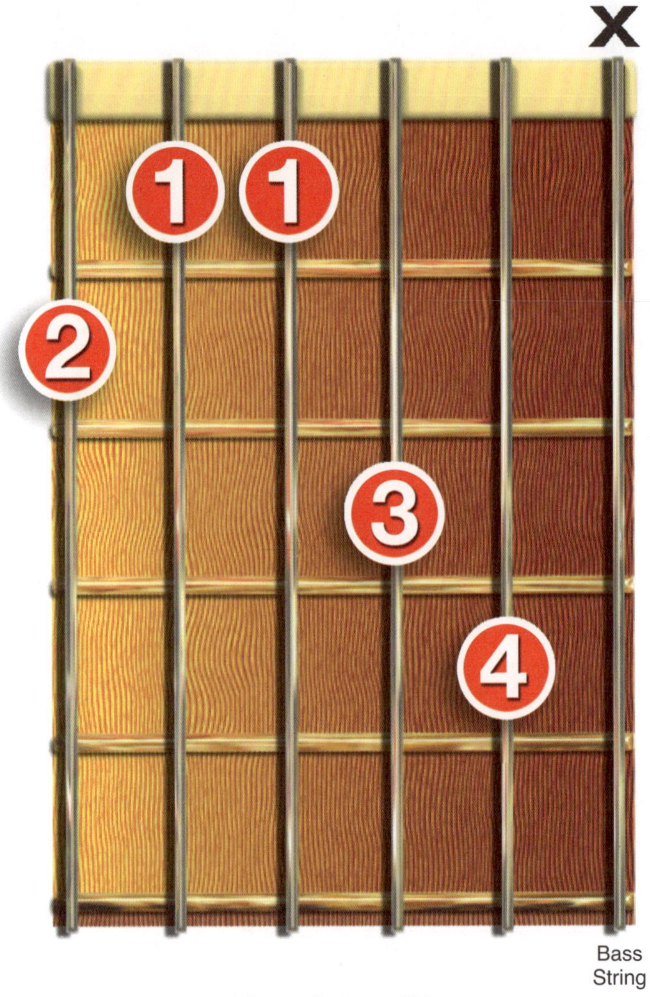

Chord Spelling

1st (C♯), 3rd (E♯), 5th (G♯), 7th (B♯), 9th (D♯), 11th (F♯)

C♯/D♭maj13

Major 13th

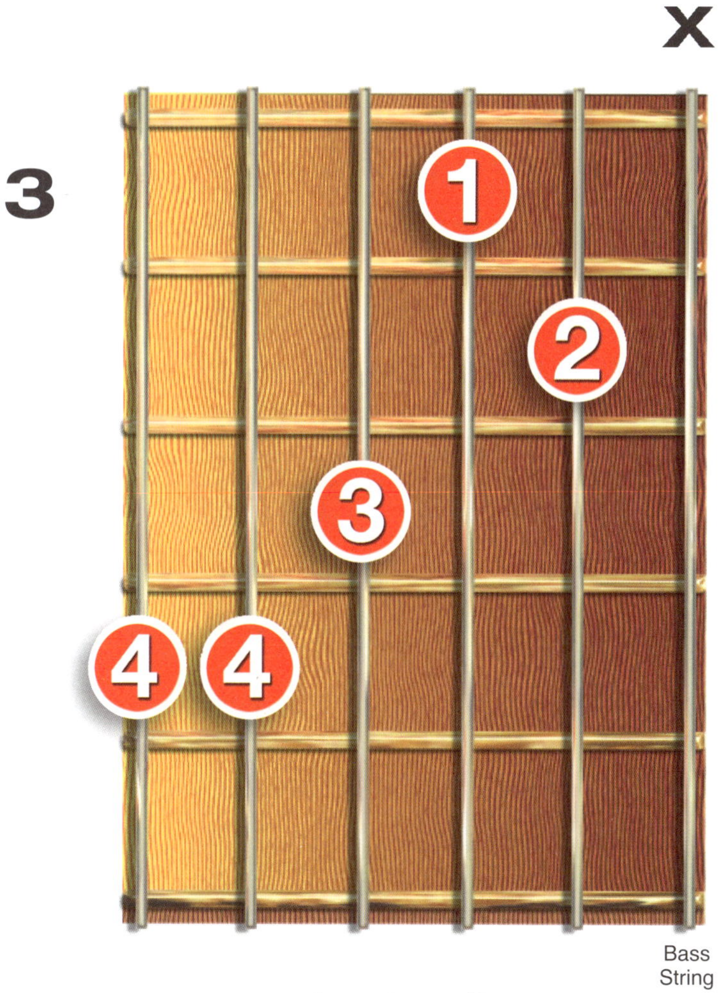

Chord Spelling

1st (C♯), 3rd (E♯), 5th (G♯), 7th (B♯), 9th (D♯), 11th (F♯), 13th (A♯)

FREE ACCESS on smartphones including iPhone & Android

Using any QR code app scan and **HEAR** the chord

D
Major

Chord Spelling

1st (D), 3rd (F♯), 5th (A)

FREE ACCESS on smartphones including iPhone & Android

Using any QR code app scan and **HEAR** the chord

Dm

Minor

O X X
1
2
3
Bass String

Chord Spelling

1st (D), ♭3rd (F), 5th (A)

FREE ACCESS on smartphones including iPhone & Android

Using any QR code app scan and **HEAR** the chord

D+

Augmented Triad

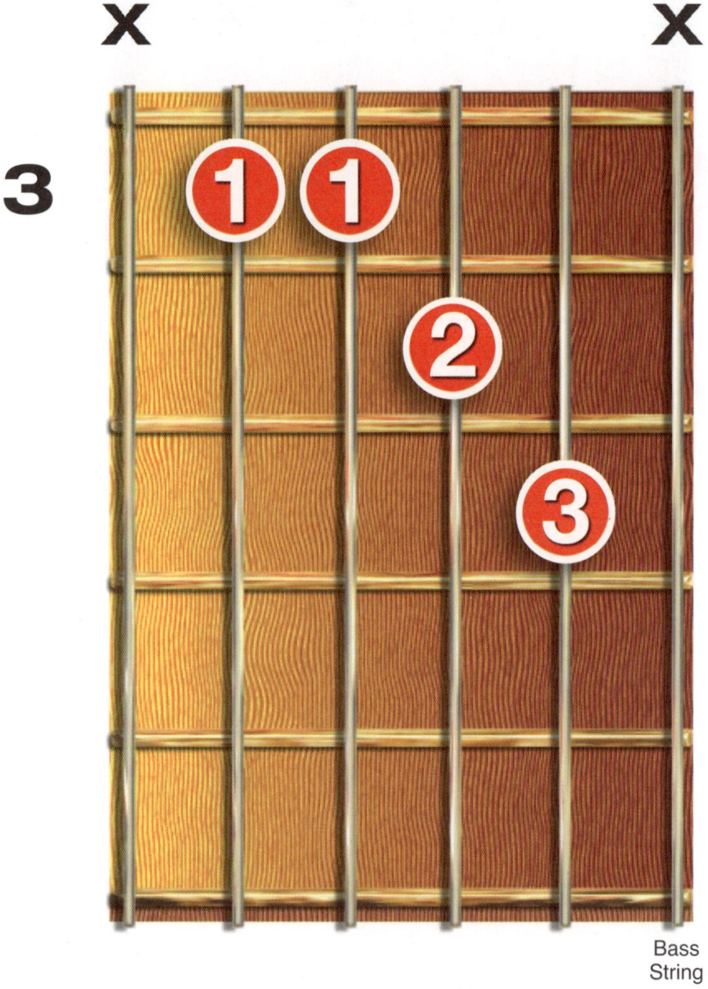
X
X
3
1
1
2
3
Bass
String

Chord Spelling

1st (D), 3rd (F♯), ♯5th (A♯)

FREE ACCESS on smartphones including iPhone & Android

Using any QR code app scan and **HEAR** the chord

D°
Diminished Triad

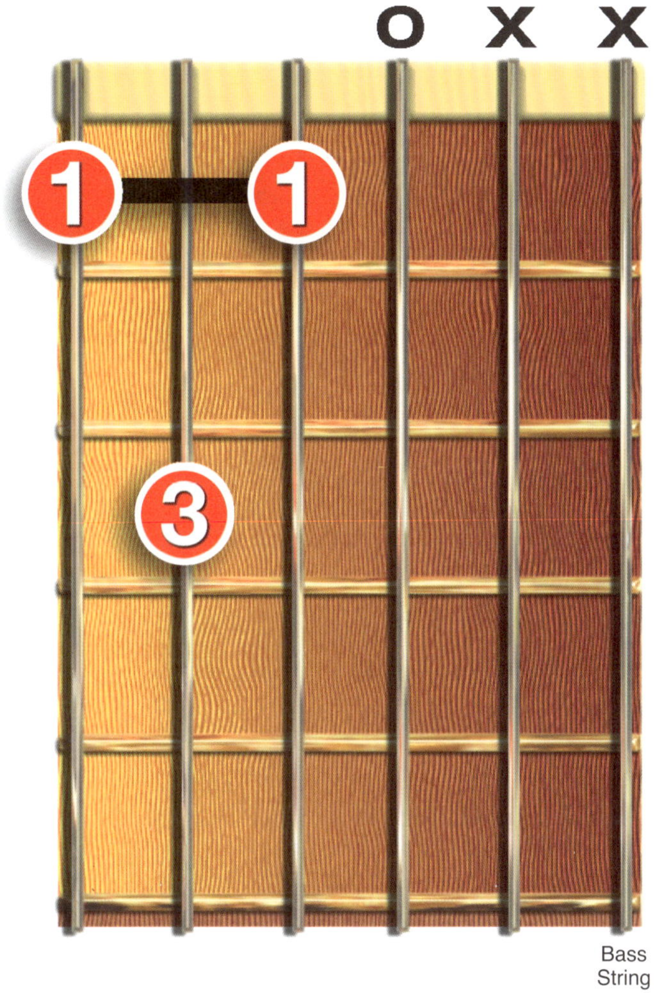

Chord Spelling

1st (D), ♭3rd (F), ♭5th (A♭)

FREE ACCESS on smartphones including iPhone & Android

Using any QR code app scan and **HEAR** the chord

Dsus2

Suspended 2nd

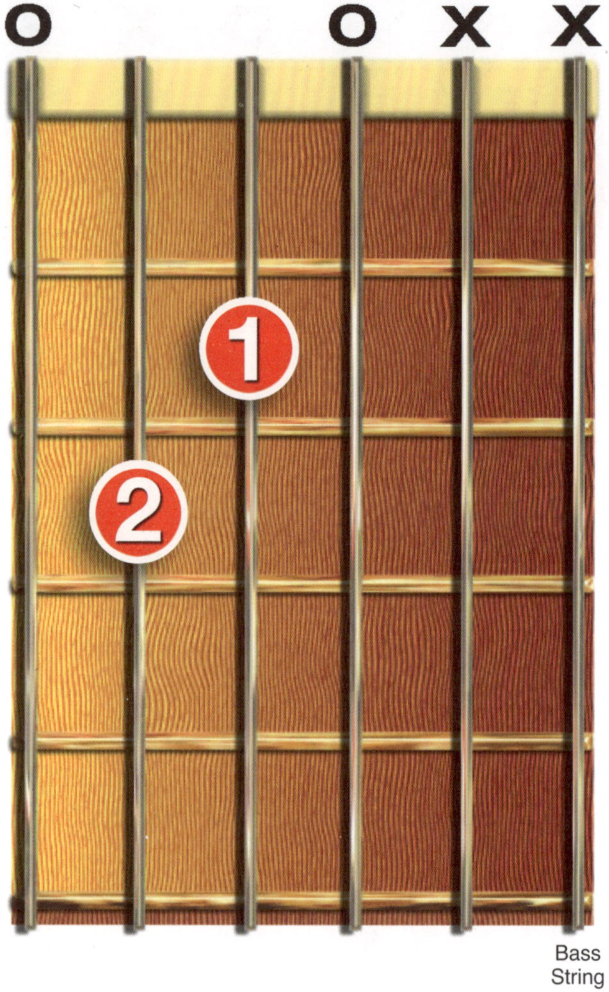

Chord Spelling

1st (D), 2nd (E), 5th (A)

FREE ACCESS on smartphones including iPhone & Android

Using any QR code app scan and **HEAR** the chord

Dsus4

Suspended 4th

Chord Spelling

1st (D), 4th (G), 5th (A)

D5

5th (Power Chord)

Chord Spelling

1st (D), 5th (A)

FREE ACCESS on smartphones including iPhone & Android

Using any QR code app scan and **HEAR** the chord

D6

Major 6th

Chord Spelling

1st (D), 3rd (F♯), 5th (A), 6th (B)

FREE ACCESS on smartphones including iPhone & Android

Using any QR code app scan and **HEAR** the chord

Dm6

Minor 6th

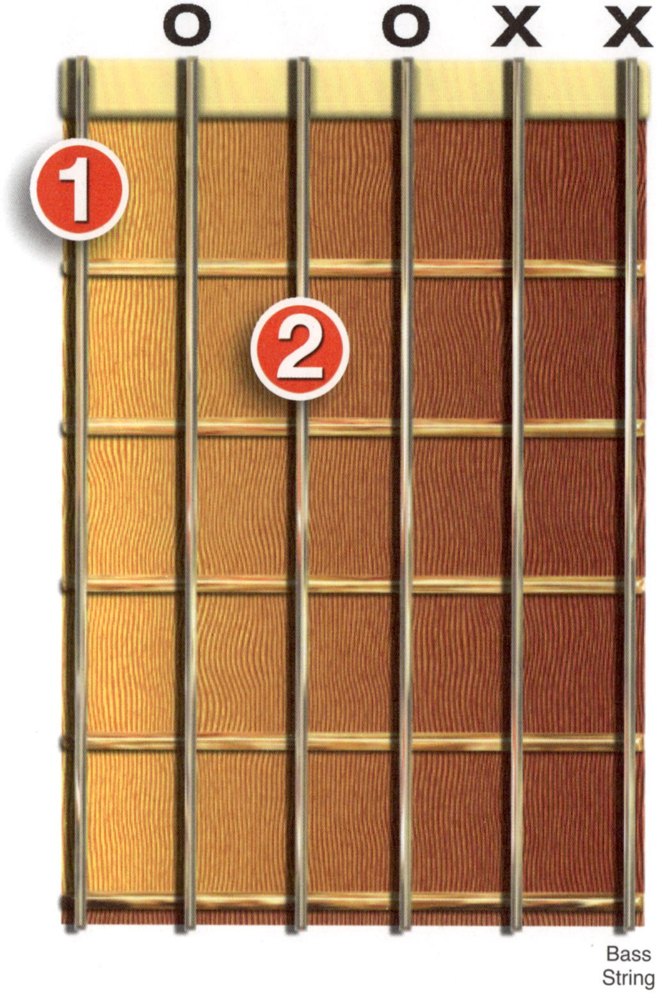

Chord Spelling

1st (D), ♭3rd (F), 5th (A), 6th (B)

D6sus4

6th Suspended 4th

Chord Spelling

1st (D), 4th (G), 5th (A), 6th (B)

FREE ACCESS on smartphones including iPhone & Android

Using any QR code app scan and **HEAR** the chord

Dmaj7

Major 7th

Chord Spelling

1st (D), 3rd (F♯), 5th (A), 7th (C♯)

FREE ACCESS on smartphones including iPhone & Android

Using any QR code app scan and **HEAR** the chord

Dm7

Minor 7th

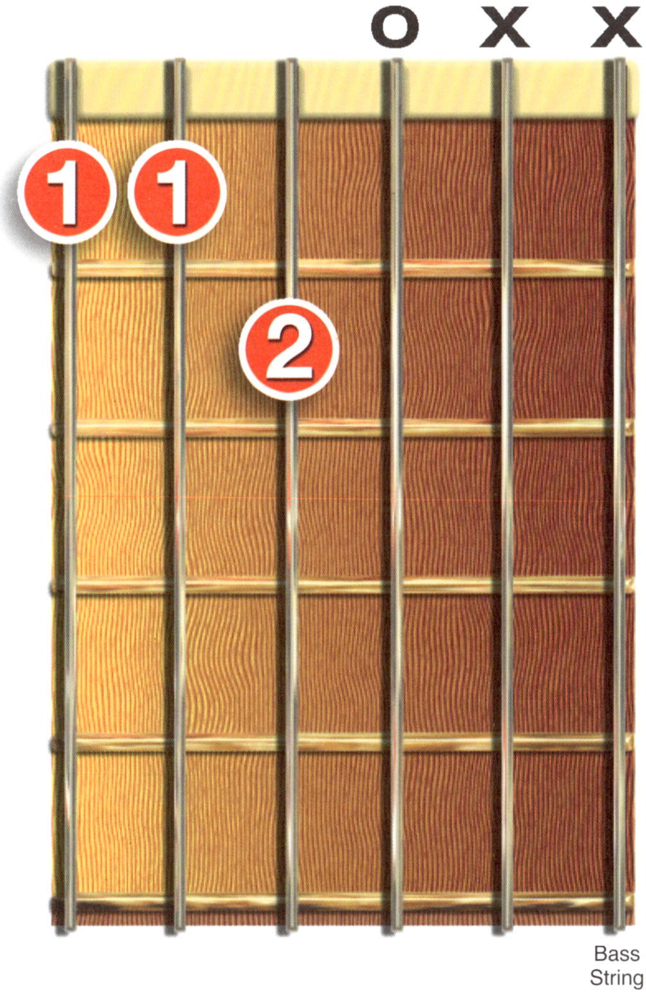

Chord Spelling

1st (D), ♭3rd (F), 5th (A), ♭7th (C)

FREE ACCESS on smartphones including iPhone & Android

Using any QR code app scan and **HEAR** the chord

D7

Dominant 7th

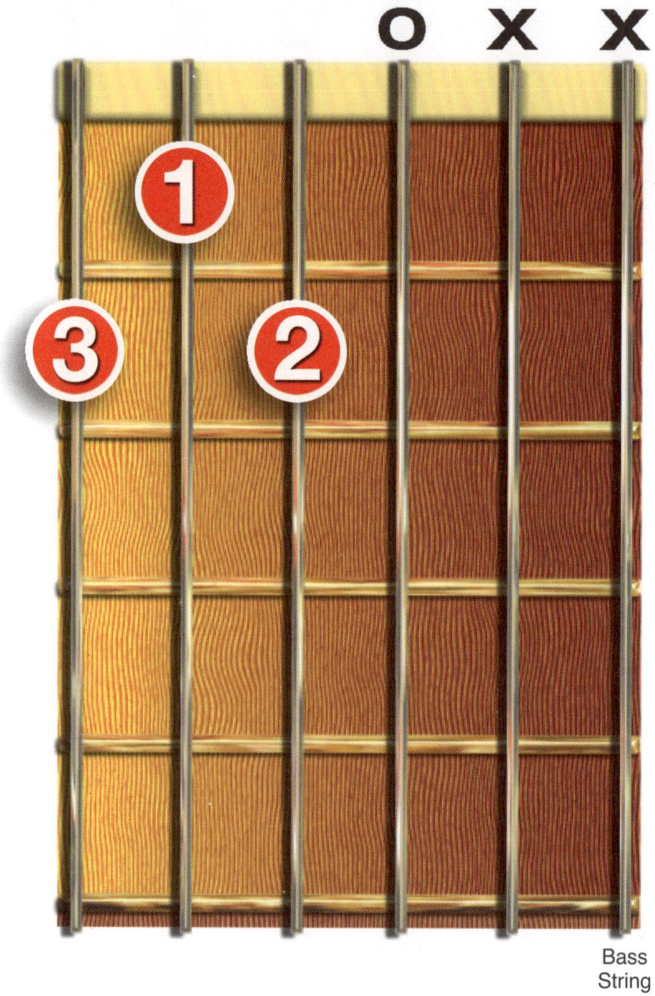

Chord Spelling

1st (D), 3rd (F♯), 5th (A), ♭7th (C)

FREE ACCESS on smartphones including iPhone & Android

Using any QR code app scan and **HEAR** the chord

D°7

Diminished 7th

Chord Spelling

1st (D), ♭3rd (F), ♭5th (A♭), ♭♭7th (B)

FREE ACCESS on smartphones including iPhone & Android

Using any QR code app scan and **HEAR** the chord

D7sus4

Dominant 7th Suspended 4th

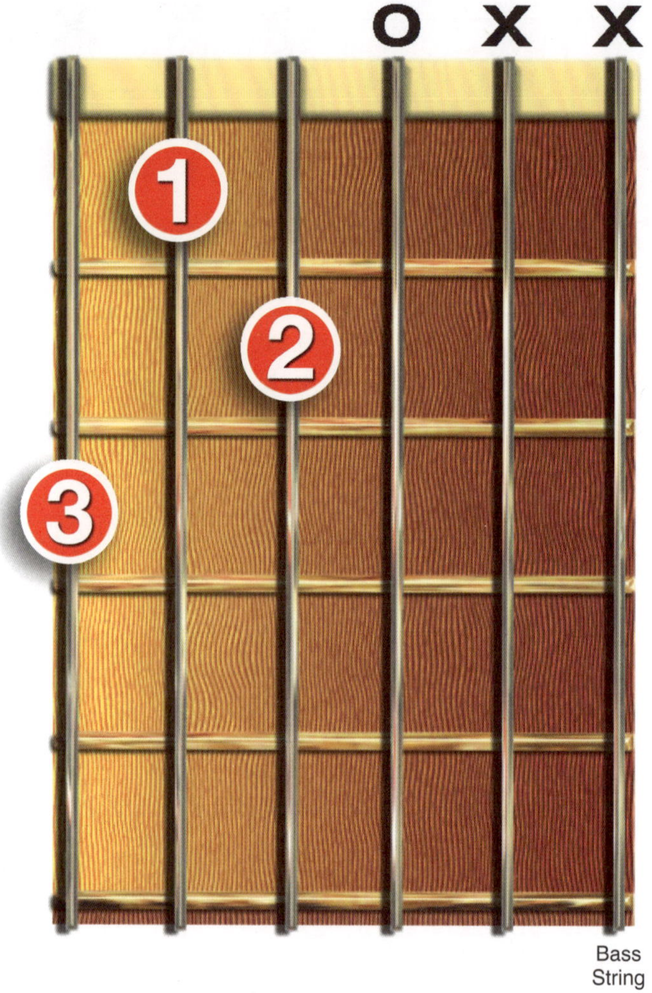

Chord Spelling

1st (D), 4th (G), 5th (A), ♭7th (C)

FREE ACCESS on smartphones including iPhone & Android

Using any QR code app scan and **HEAR** the chord

Dmaj9

Major 9th

X
X
6
1
3
2
4
Bass
String

Chord Spelling

1st (D), 3rd (F♯), 5th (A), 7th (C♯), 9th (E)

FREE ACCESS on smartphones including iPhone & Android

Using any QR code app scan and **HEAR** the chord

Dm9

Minor 9th

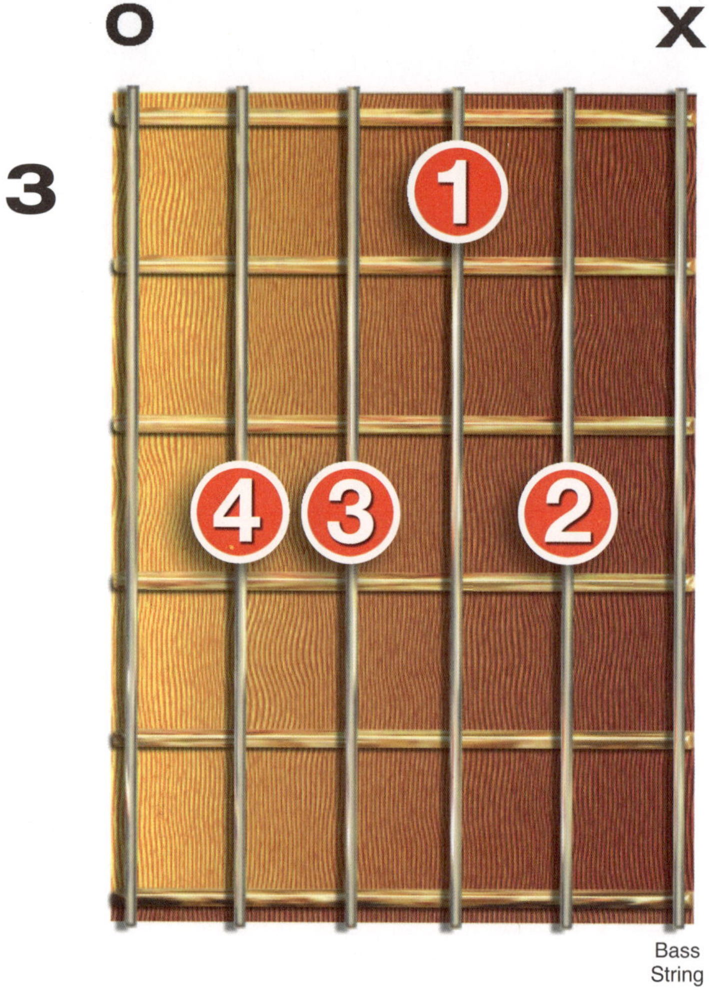

Chord Spelling

1st (D), ♭3rd (F), 5th (A), ♭7th (C), 9th (E)

FREE ACCESS on smartphones including iPhone & Android

Using any QR code app scan and **HEAR** the chord

D9

Dominant 9th

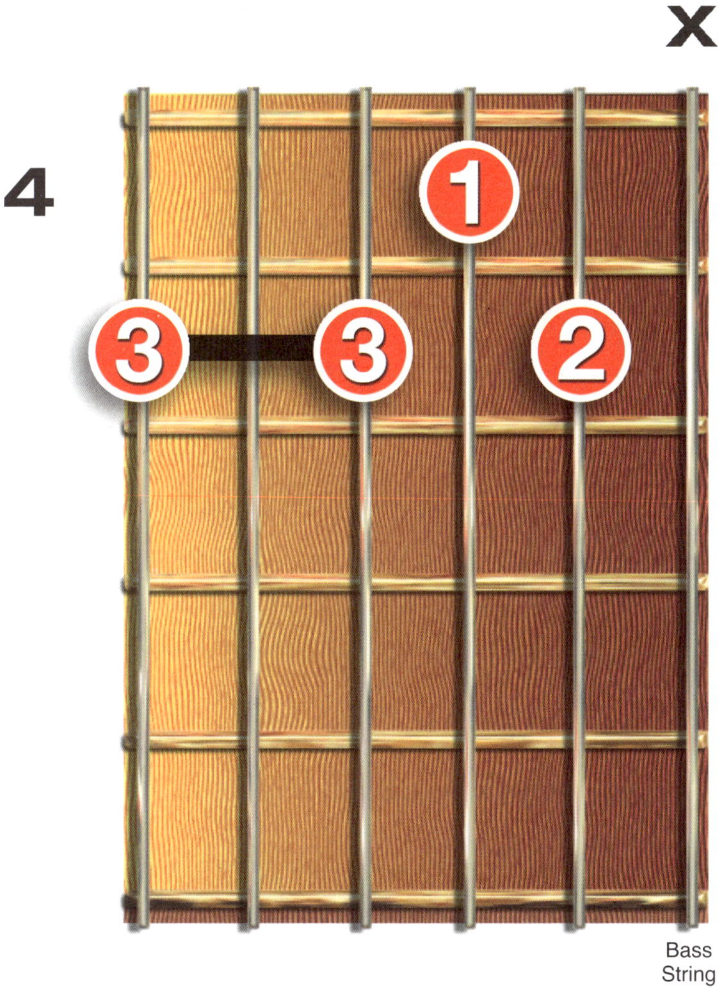

Chord Spelling

1st (D), 3rd (F♯), 5th (A), ♭7th (C), 9th (E)

FREE ACCESS on smartphones including iPhone & Android

Using any QR code app scan and **HEAR** the chord

Dmaj11

Major 11th

Chord Spelling

1st (D), 3rd (F♯), 5th (A), 7th (C♯), 9th (E), 11th (G)

FREE ACCESS on smartphones including iPhone & Android

Using any QR code app scan and **HEAR** the chord

Dmaj13

Major 13th

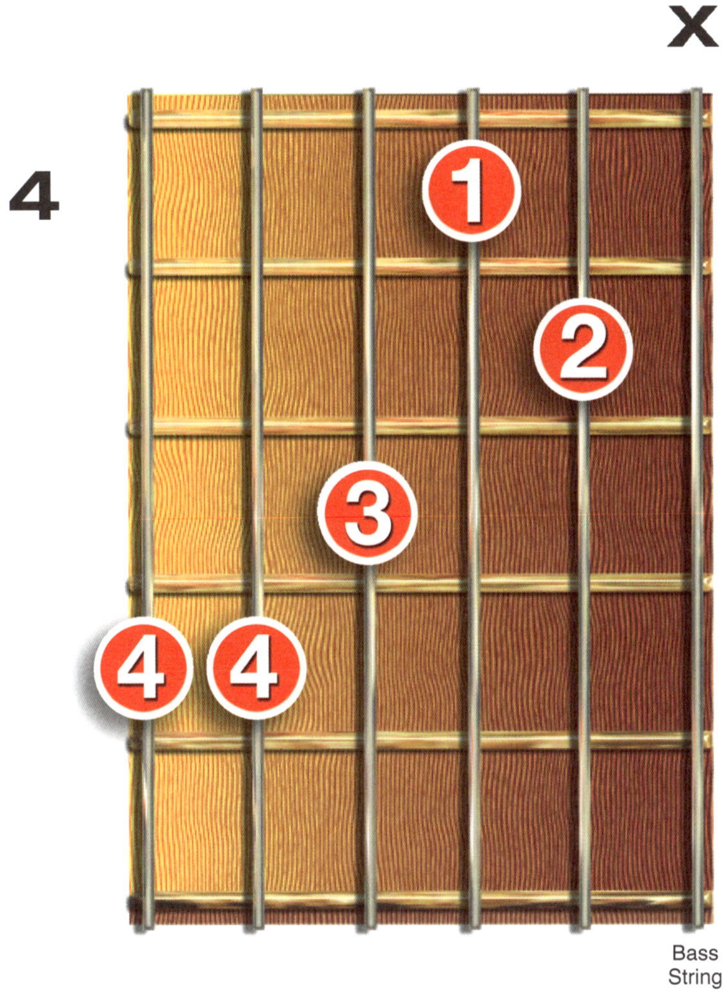

Chord Spelling

1st (D), 3rd (F♯), 5th (A), 7th (C♯), 9th (E), 11th (G), 13th (B)

FREE ACCESS on smartphones including iPhone & Android

Using any QR code app scan and **HEAR** the chord

D♯/E♭
Major

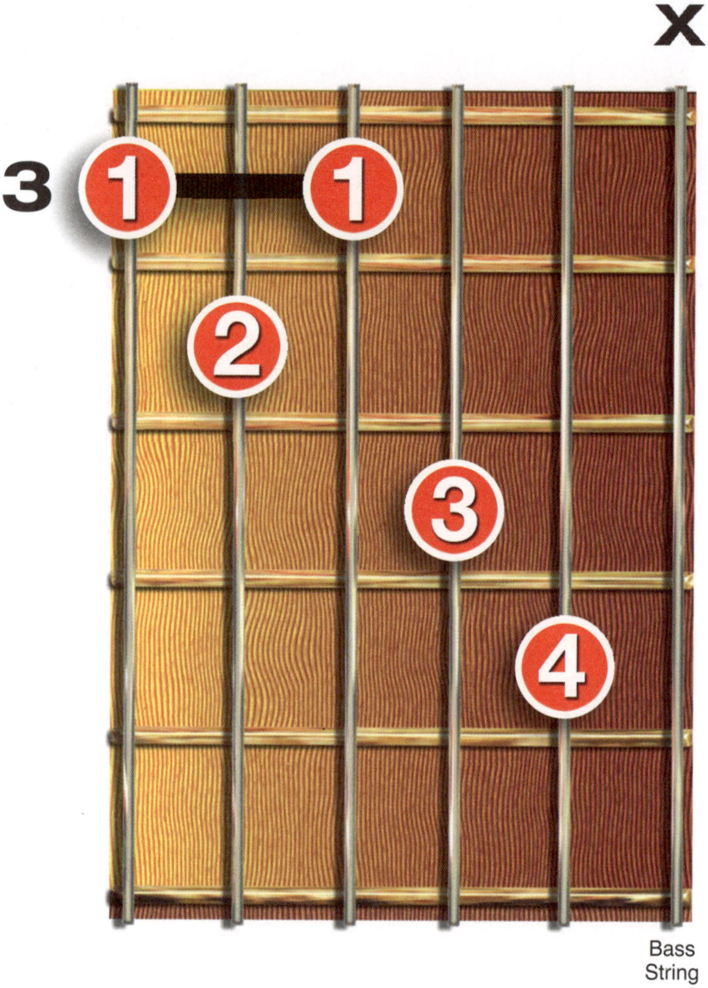

Chord Spelling

1st (E♭), 3rd (G), 5th (B♭)

D♯/E♭m

Minor

Chord Spelling

1st (E♭), ♭3rd (G♭), 5th (B♭)

FREE ACCESS on smartphones including iPhone & Android

Using any QR code app scan and **HEAR** the chord

D♯/E♭+
Augmented Triad

Chord Spelling

1st (E♭), 3rd (G), ♯5th (B)

FREE ACCESS on smartphones including iPhone & Android

Using any QR code app scan and **HEAR** the chord

D♯/E♭°
Diminished Triad

Chord Spelling

1st (E♭), ♭3rd (G♭), ♭5th (B♭♭)

FREE ACCESS on smartphones including iPhone & Android

Using any QR code app scan and **HEAR** the chord

D♯/E♭sus2

Suspended 2nd

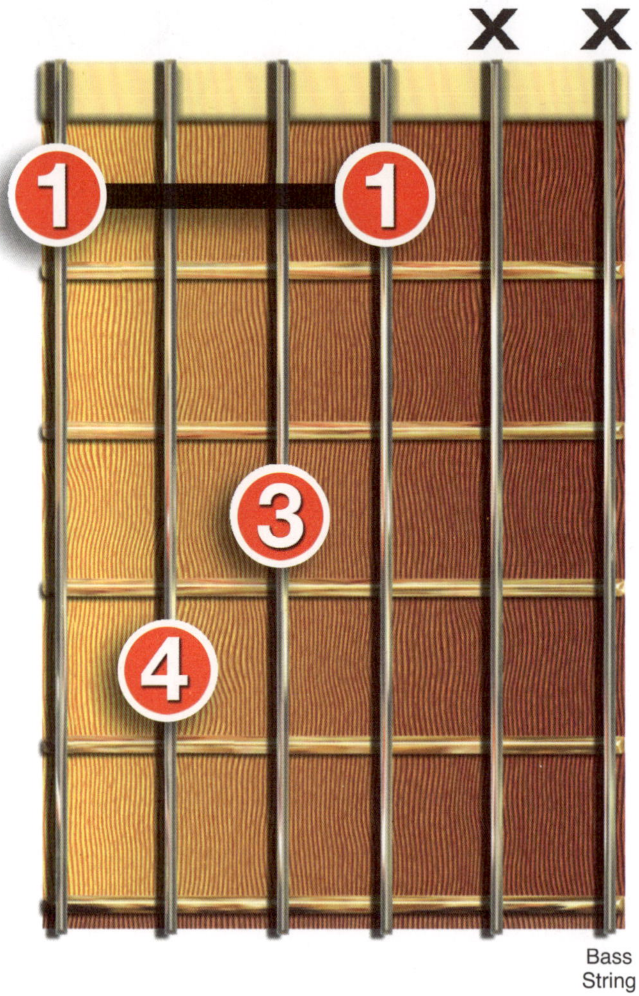

X X
1
1
3
4
Bass
String

Chord Spelling

1st (E♭), 2nd (F), 5th (B♭)

FREE ACCESS on smartphones including iPhone & Android

Using any QR code app scan and **HEAR** the chord

D♯/E♭sus4

Suspended 4th

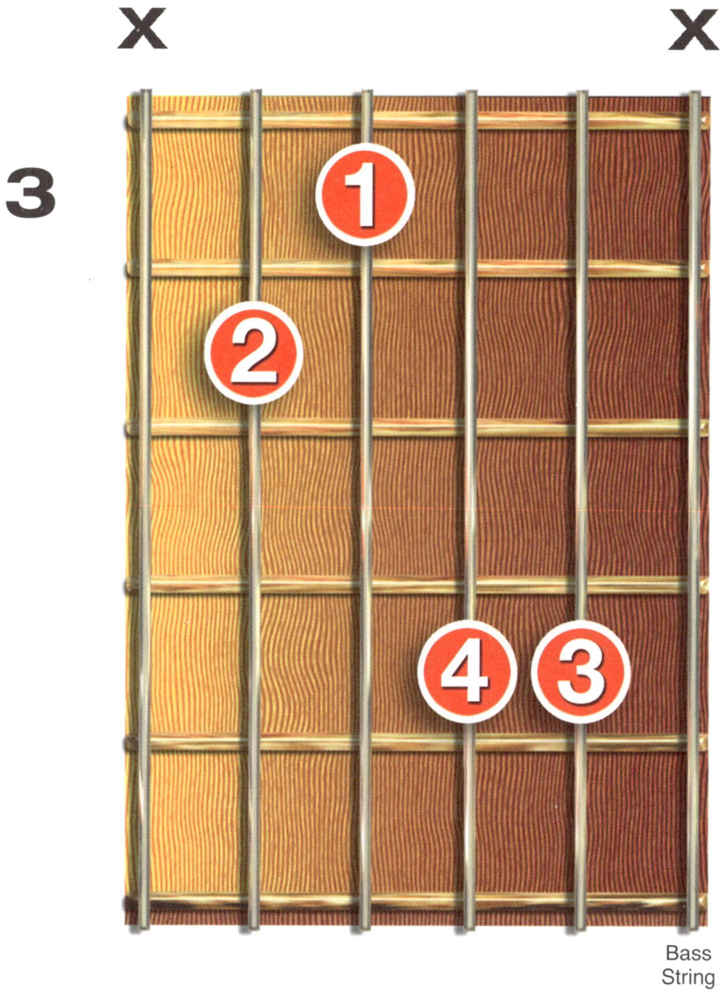

X
X
3
1
2
4
3
Bass String

Chord Spelling

1st (E♭), 4th (A♭), 5th (B♭)

D♯/E♭5

5th (Power Chord)

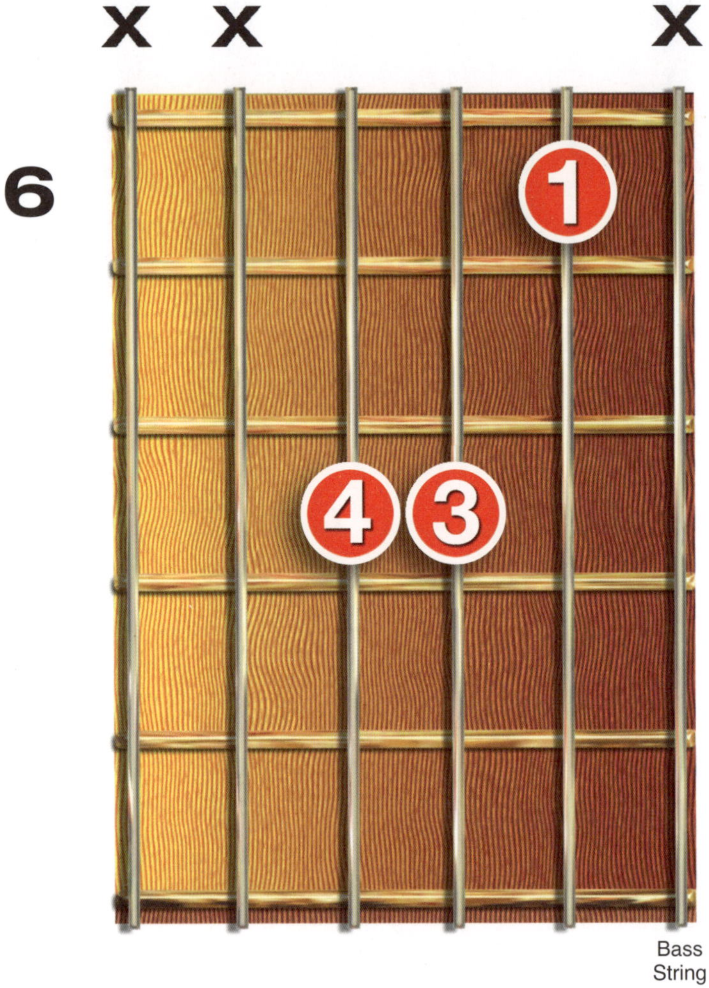
X X X
6
1
4 3
Bass
String

Chord Spelling

1st (E♭), 5th (B♭)

FREE ACCESS on smartphones including iPhone & Android

Using any QR code app scan and **HEAR** the chord

D♯/E♭6

Major 6th

Chord Spelling

1st (E♭), 3rd (G), 5th (B♭), 6th (C)

FREE ACCESS on smartphones including iPhone & Android

Using any QR code app scan and **HEAR** the chord

D♯/E♭m6

Minor 6th

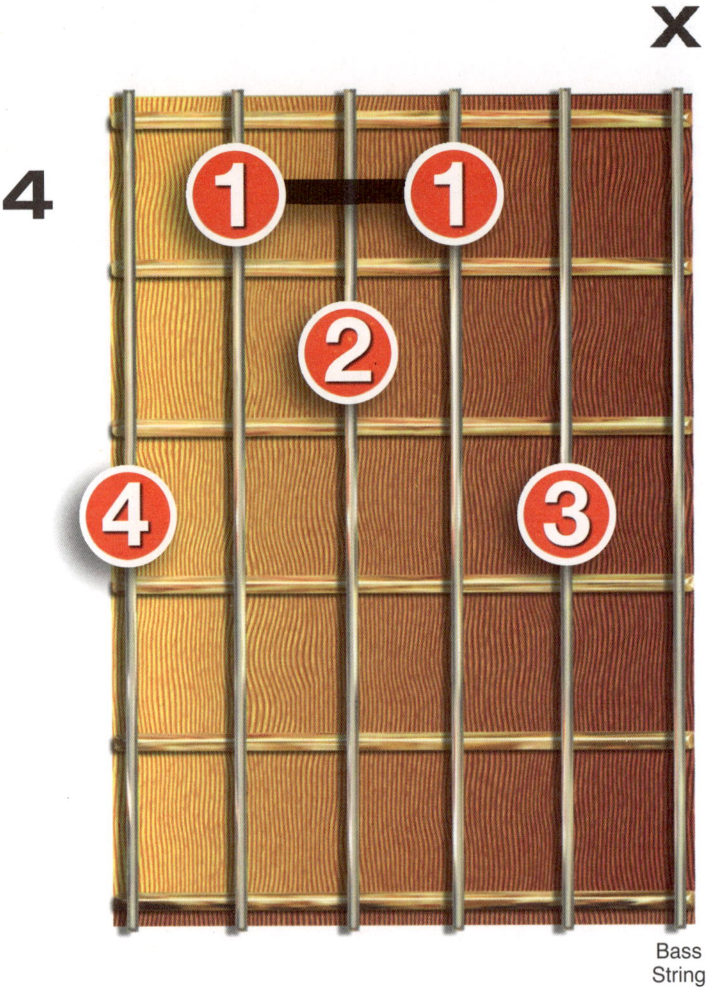

Chord Spelling

1st (E♭), ♭3rd (G♭), 5th (B♭), 6th (C)

FREE ACCESS on smartphones including iPhone & Android

Using any QR code app scan and **HEAR** the chord

D♯/E♭6sus4

6th Suspended 4th

Chord Spelling

1st (E♭), 4th (A♭), 5th (B♭), 6th (C)

FREE ACCESS on smartphones including iPhone & Android

Using any QR code app scan and **HEAR** the chord

D♯/E♭maj7

Major 7th

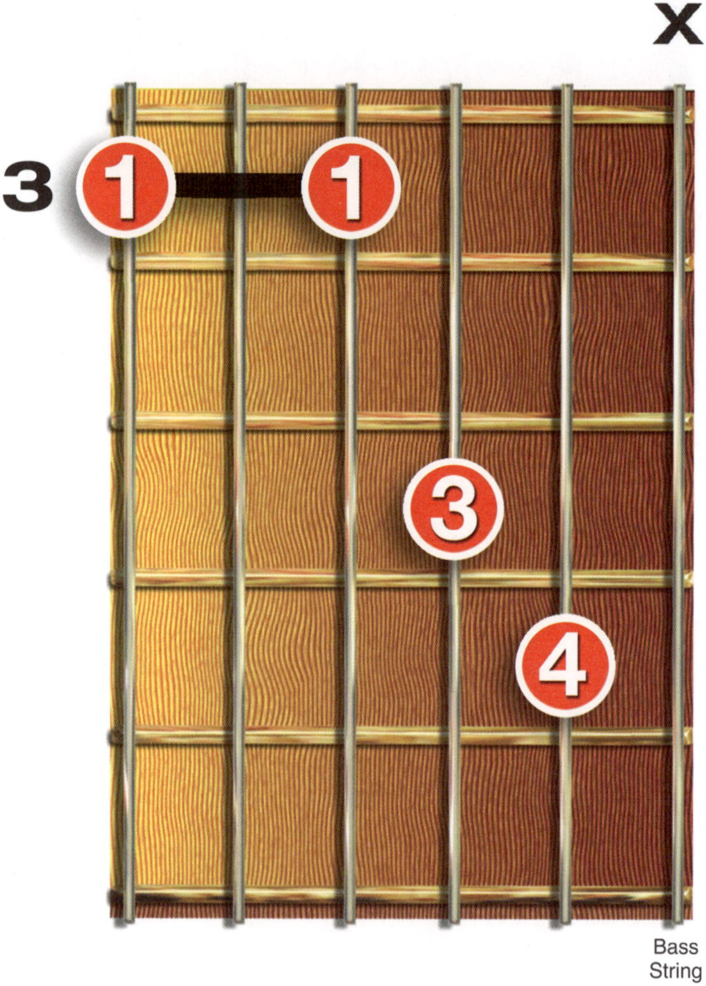

Chord Spelling

1st (E♭), 3rd (G), 5th (B♭), 7th (D)

FREE ACCESS on smartphones including iPhone & Android

Using any QR code app scan and **HEAR** the chord

D♯/E♭m7

Minor 7th

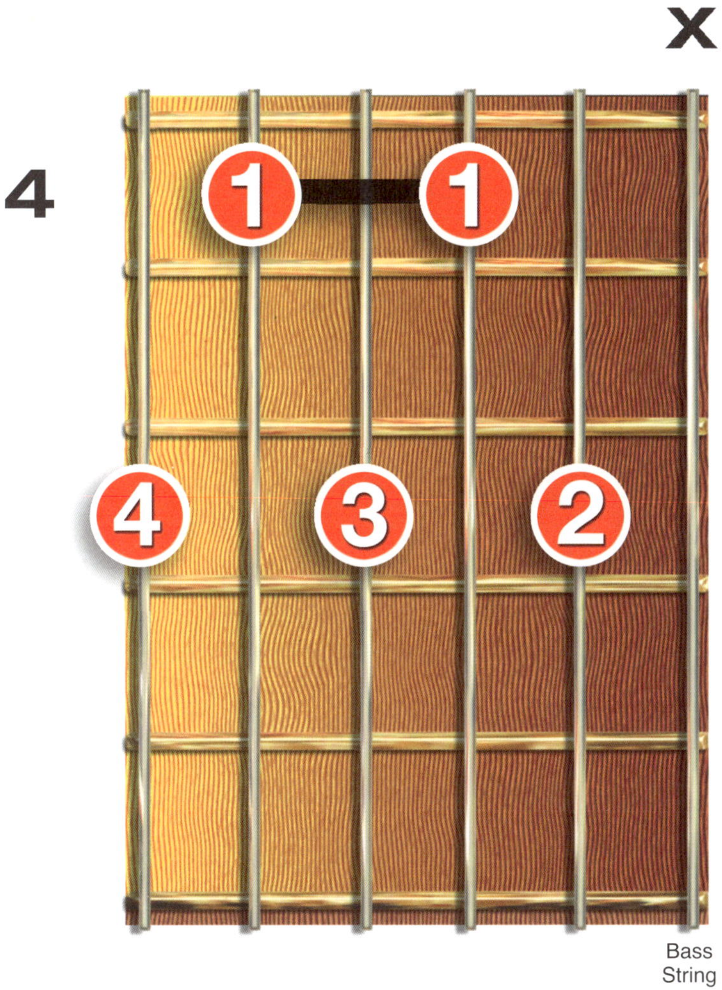
x
4
1
1
4
3
2
Bass String

Chord Spelling

1st (E♭), ♭3rd (G♭), 5th (B♭), ♭7th (D♭)

FREE ACCESS on smartphones including iPhone & Android

Using any QR code app scan and **HEAR** the chord

D♯/E♭7

Dominant 7th

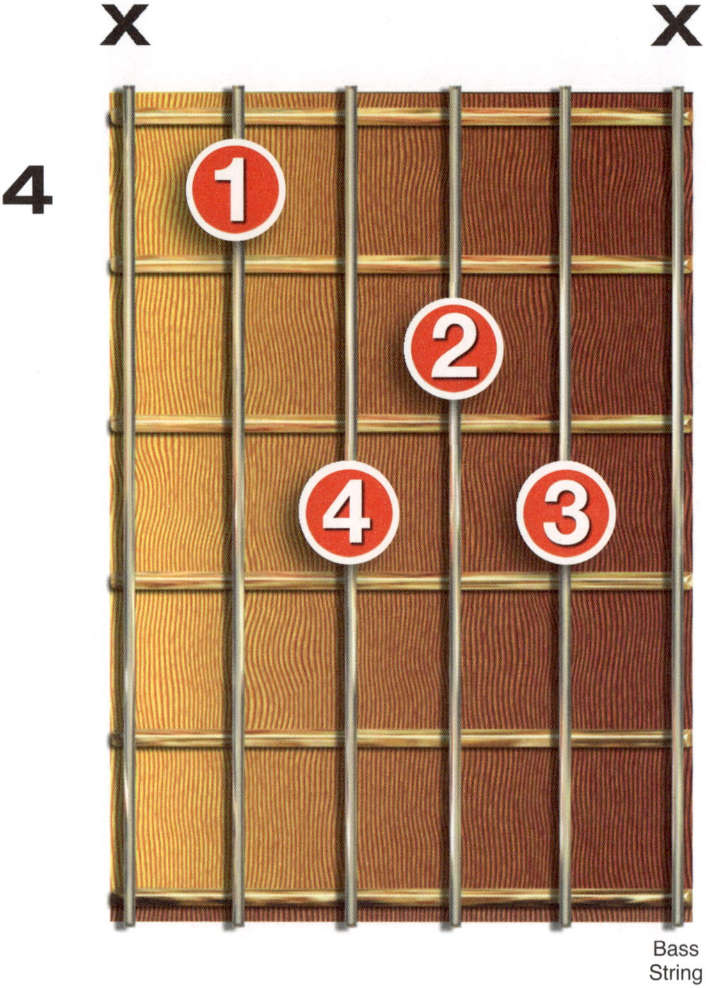
X
X
4
1
2
4
3
Bass String

Chord Spelling

1st (E♭), 3rd (G), 5th (B♭), ♭7th (D♭)

FREE ACCESS on smartphones including iPhone & Android

Using any QR code app scan and **HEAR** the chord

D♯/E♭°7
Diminished 7th

X X
2
1
4
3
Bass String

Chord Spelling

1st (E♭), ♭3rd (G♭), ♭5th (B♭♭), ♭♭7th (D♭♭)

FREE ACCESS on smartphones including iPhone & Android

Using any QR code app scan and **HEAR** the chord

D♯/E♭7sus4

Dominant 7th Suspended 4th

Chord Spelling

1st (E♭), 4th (A♭), 5th (B♭), ♭7th (D♭)

FREE ACCESS on smartphones including iPhone & Android

Using any QR code app scan and **HEAR** the chord

A
A♯/B♭
B
C
C♯/D♭
D
D♯/E♭
E
F
F♯/G♭
G
G♯/A♭

D♯/E♭maj9

Major 9th

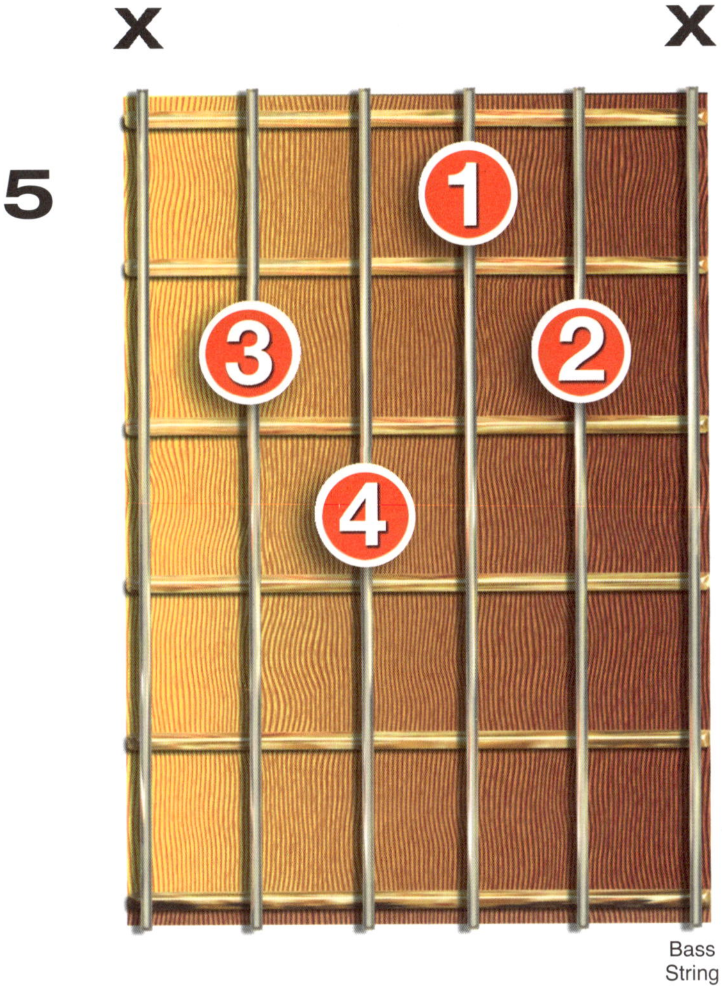

Chord Spelling

1st (E♭), 3rd (G), 5th (B♭), 7th (D), 9th (F)

FREE ACCESS on smartphones including iPhone & Android

Using any QR code app scan and **HEAR** the chord

D♯/E♭m9

Minor 9th

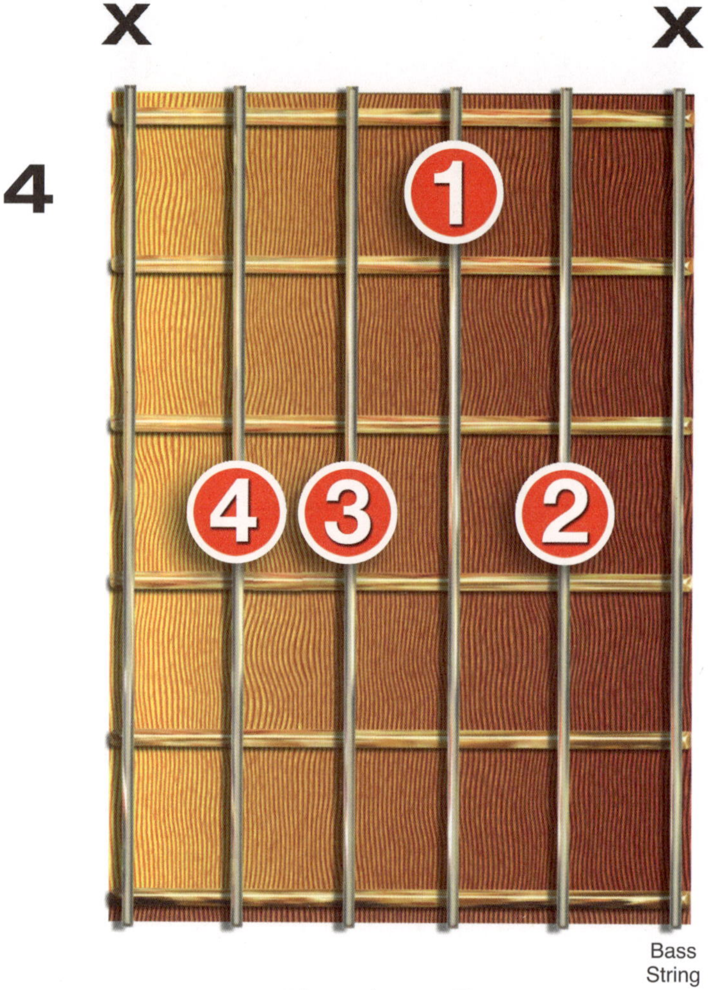

Chord Spelling

1st (E♭), ♭3rd (G♭), 5th (B♭), ♭7th (D♭), 9th (F)

FREE ACCESS on smartphones including iPhone & Android

Using any QR code app scan and **HEAR** the chord

D♯/E♭9

Dominant 9th

Chord Spelling

1st (E♭), 3rd (G), 5th (B♭), ♭7th (D♭), 9th (F)

FREE ACCESS on smartphones including iPhone & Android

Using any QR code app scan and **HEAR** the chord

A
A♯/B♭
B
C
C♯/D♭
D
D♯/E♭
E
F
F♯/G♭
G
G♯/A♭

D♯/E♭maj11

Major 11th

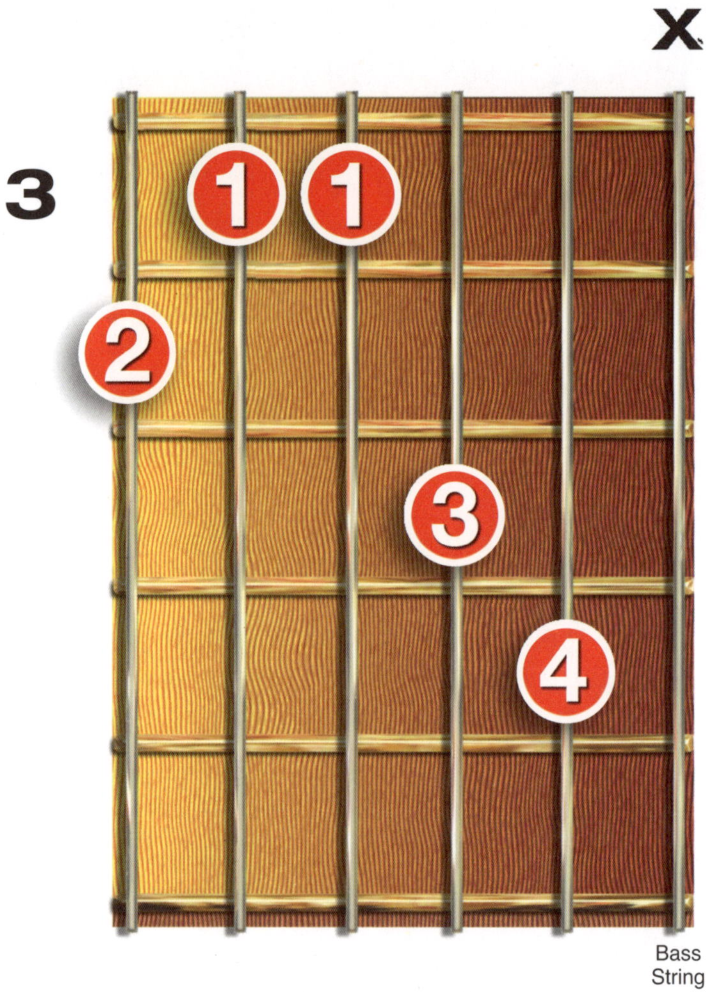

Chord Spelling

1st (E♭), 3rd (G), 5th (B♭), 7th (D), 9th (F), 11th (A♭)

FREE ACCESS on smartphones including iPhone & Android

Using any QR code app scan and **HEAR** the chord

D♯/E♭maj13

Major 13th

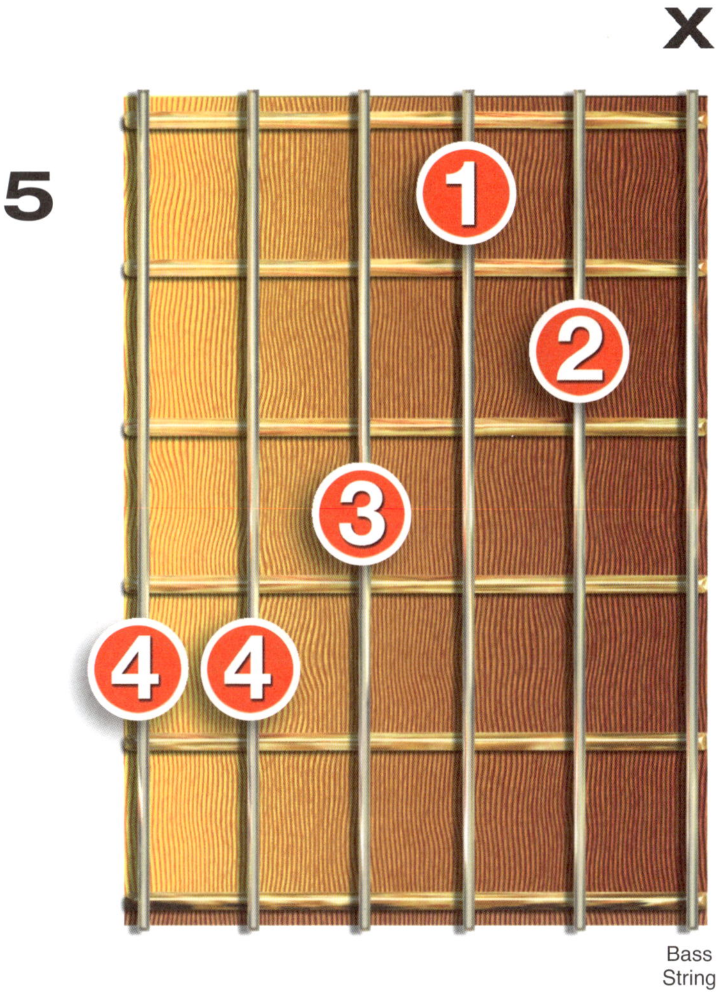

Chord Spelling

1st (E♭), 3rd (G), 5th (B♭), 7th (D), 9th (F), 11th (A♭), 13th (C)

A
A♯/B♭
B
C
C♯/D♭
D
D♯/E♭
E
F
F♯/G♭
G
G♯/A♭

A
A♯/B♭
B
C
C♯/D♭
D
D♯/E♭
E
F
F♯/G♭
G
G♯/A♭

E
Major

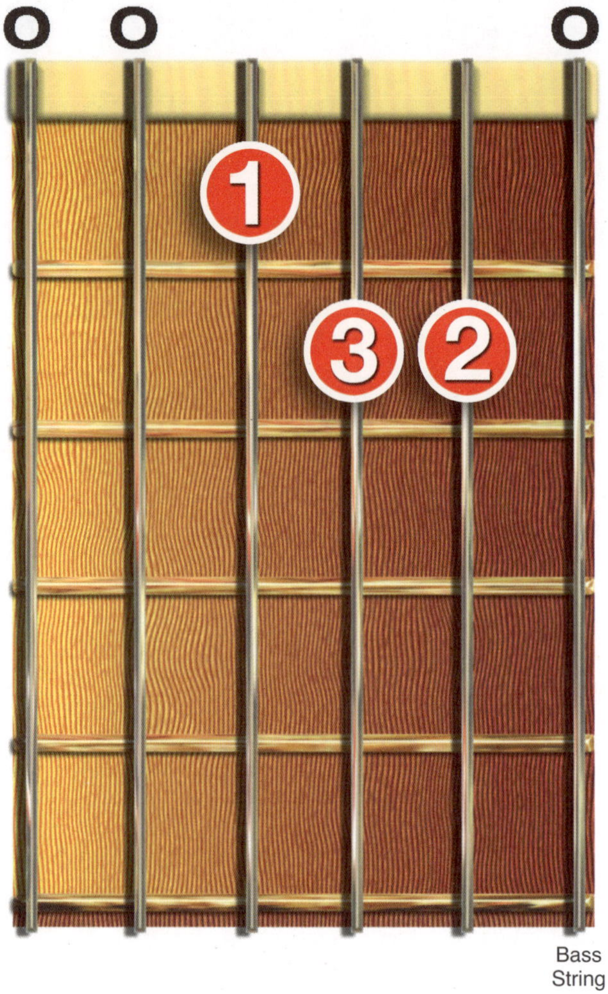

Chord Spelling

1st (E), 3rd (G♯), 5th (B)

FREE ACCESS on smartphones including iPhone & Android

Using any QR code app scan and **HEAR** the chord

Em

Minor

Chord Spelling

1st (E), ♭3rd (G), 5th (B)

FREE ACCESS on smartphones including iPhone & Android

Using any QR code app scan and **HEAR** the chord

A
A♯/B♭
B
C
C♯/D♭
D
D♯/E♭
E
F
F♯/G♭
G
G♯/A♭

E+

Augmented Triad

Chord Spelling

1st (E), 3rd (G♯), ♯5th (B♯)

FREE ACCESS on smartphones including iPhone & Android

Using any QR code app scan and **HEAR** the chord

E°

Diminished Triad

Chord Spelling

1st (E), ♭3rd (G), ♭5th (B♭)

FREE ACCESS on smartphones including iPhone & Android

Using any QR code app scan and **HEAR** the chord

Esus2

Suspended 2nd

Chord Spelling

1st (E), 2nd (F♯), 5th (B)

Esus4

Suspended 4th

Chord Spelling

1st (E), 4th (A), 5th (B)

E5

5th (Power Chord)

Chord Spelling

1st (E), 5th (B)

FREE ACCESS on smartphones including iPhone & Android

Using any QR code app scan and **HEAR** the chord

E6

Major 6th

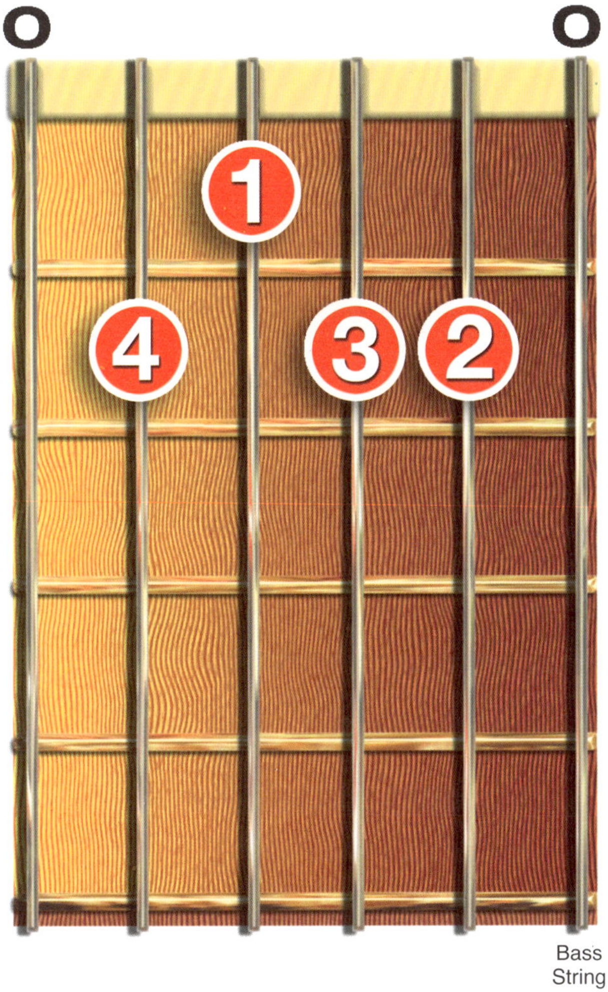

Chord Spelling

1st (E), 3rd (G♯), 5th (B), 6th (C♯)

FREE ACCESS on smartphones including iPhone & Android

Using any QR code app scan and **HEAR** the chord

Em6

Minor 6th

Chord Spelling

1st (E), ♭3rd (G), 5th (B), 6th (C♯)

FREE ACCESS on smartphones including iPhone & Android

Using any QR code app scan and **HEAR** the chord

E6sus4

6th Suspended 4th

Bass String

Chord Spelling

1st (E), 4th (A), 5th (B), 6th (C♯)

FREE ACCESS on smartphones including iPhone & Android

Using any QR code app scan and **HEAR** the chord

Emaj7

Major 7th

Chord Spelling

1st (E), 3rd (G♯), 5th (B), 7th (D♯)

FREE ACCESS on smartphones including iPhone & Android

Using any QR code app scan and **HEAR** the chord

Em7

Minor 7th

Chord Spelling

1st (E), ♭3rd (G), 5th (B), ♭7th (D)

A
A♯/B♭
B
C
C♯/D♭
D
D♯/E♭
E
F
F♯/G♭
G
G♯/A♭

FREE ACCESS on smartphones including iPhone & Android

Using any QR code app scan and **HEAR** the chord

E7

Dominant 7th

Chord Spelling

1st (E), 3rd (G♯), 5th (B), ♭7th (D)

FREE ACCESS on smartphones including iPhone & Android

Using any QR code app scan and **HEAR** the chord

E°7

Diminished 7th

Chord Spelling

1st (E), ♭3rd (G), ♭5th (B♭), ♭♭7th (D♭)

E7sus4

Dominant 7th Suspended 4th

Chord Spelling

1st (E), 4th (A), 5th (B), ♭7th (D)

FREE ACCESS on smartphones including iPhone & Android

Using any QR code app scan and **HEAR** the chord

Emaj9

Major 9th

Chord Spelling

1st (E), 3rd (G♯), 5th (B), 7th (D♯), 9th (F♯)

FREE ACCESS on smartphones including iPhone & Android

Using any QR code app scan and **HEAR** the chord

Em9

Minor 9th

Chord Spelling

1st (E), ♭3rd (G), 5th (B), ♭7th (D), 9th (F♯)

FREE ACCESS on smartphones including iPhone & Android

Using any QR code app scan and **HEAR** the chord

E9

Dominant 9th

Chord Spelling

1st (E), 3rd (G♯), 5th (B), ♭7th (D), 9th (F♯)

FREE ACCESS on smartphones including iPhone & Android

Using any QR code app scan and **HEAR** the chord

Emaj11

Major 11th

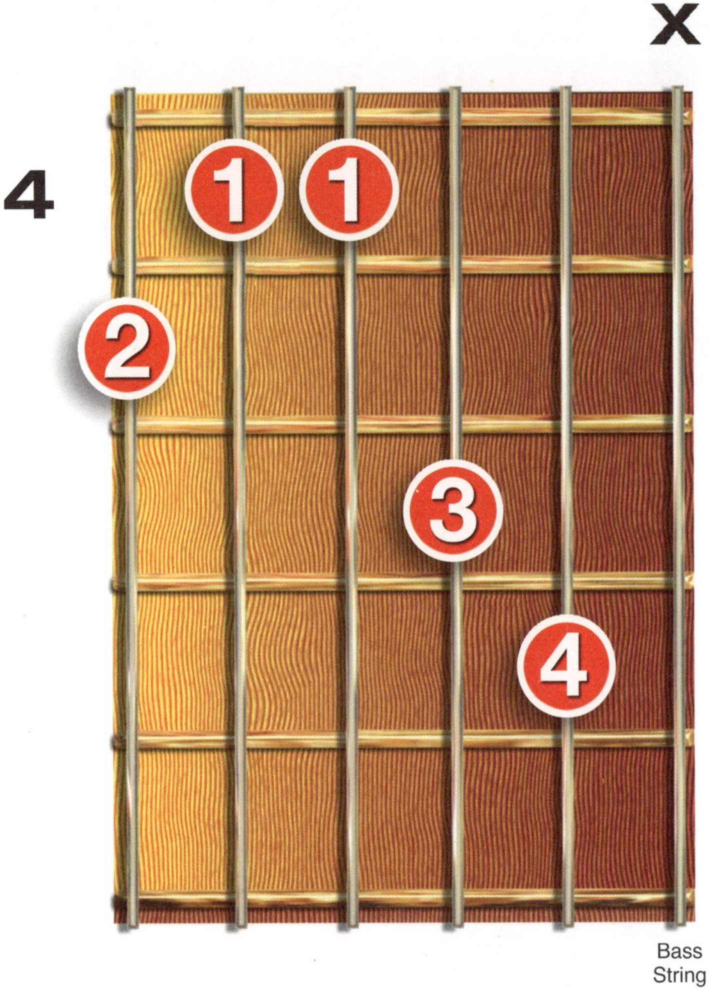

Chord Spelling

1st (E), 3rd (G♯), 5th (B), 7th (D♯), 9th (F♯), 11th (A)

Emaj13

Major 13th

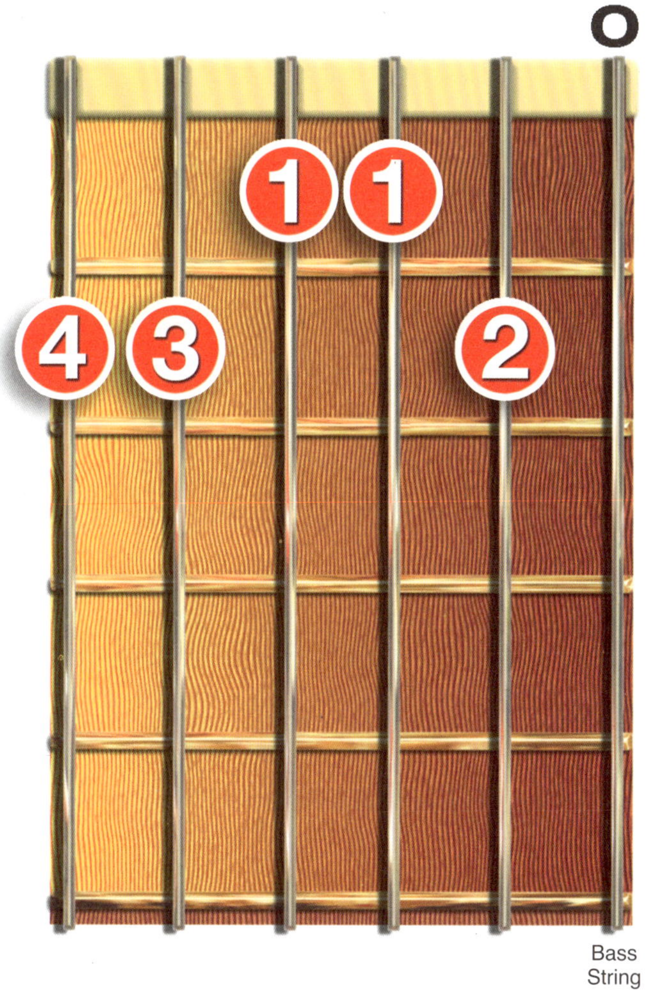

Chord Spelling

1st (E), 3rd (G♯), 5th (B), 7th (D♯), 9th (F), 11th (A), 13th (C♯)

FREE ACCESS on smartphones including iPhone & Android

Using any QR code app scan and **HEAR** the chord

F

Major

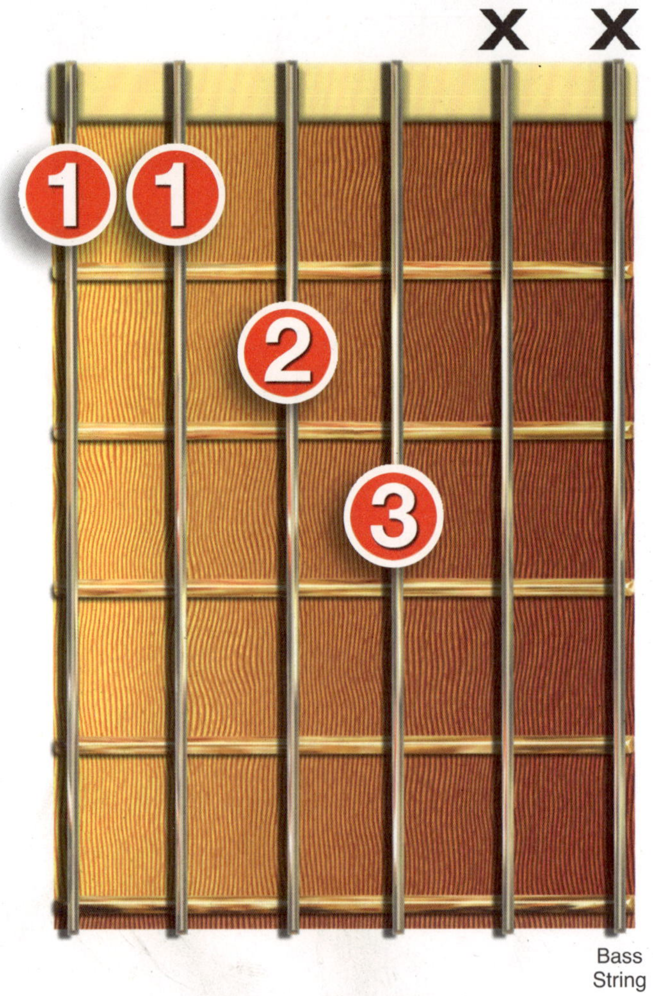

Chord Spelling

1st (F), 3rd (A), 5th (C)

FREE ACCESS on smartphones including iPhone & Android

Using any QR code app scan and **HEAR** the chord

Fm

Minor

Chord Spelling

1st (F), ♭3rd (A♭), 5th (C)

FREE ACCESS on smartphones including iPhone & Android

Using any QR code app scan and **HEAR** the chord

A
A♯/B♭
B
C
C♯/D♭
D
D♯/E♭
E
F
F♯/G♭
G
G♯/A♭

F+

Augmented Triad

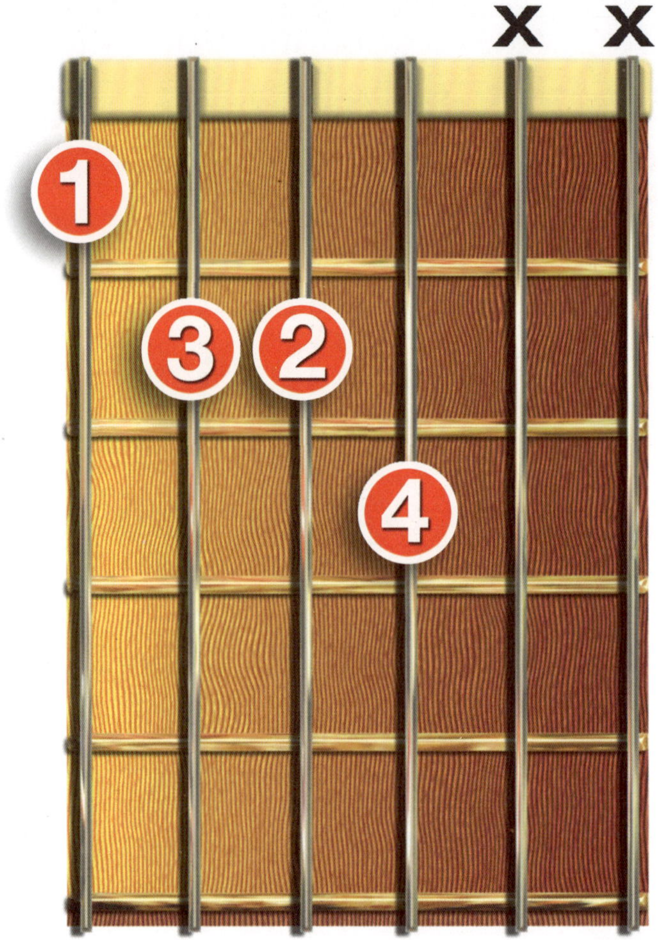
X X
1
3 2
4
Bass
String

Chord Spelling

1st (F), 3rd (A), ♯5th (C♯)

FREE ACCESS on smartphones including iPhone & Android

Using any QR code app scan and **HEAR** the chord

F°

Diminished Triad

O
X X
2
1
4
Bass String

Chord Spelling

1st (F), ♭3rd (A♭), ♭5th (C♭)

FREE ACCESS on smartphones including iPhone & Android

Using any QR code app scan and **HEAR** the chord

Fsus2

Suspended 2nd

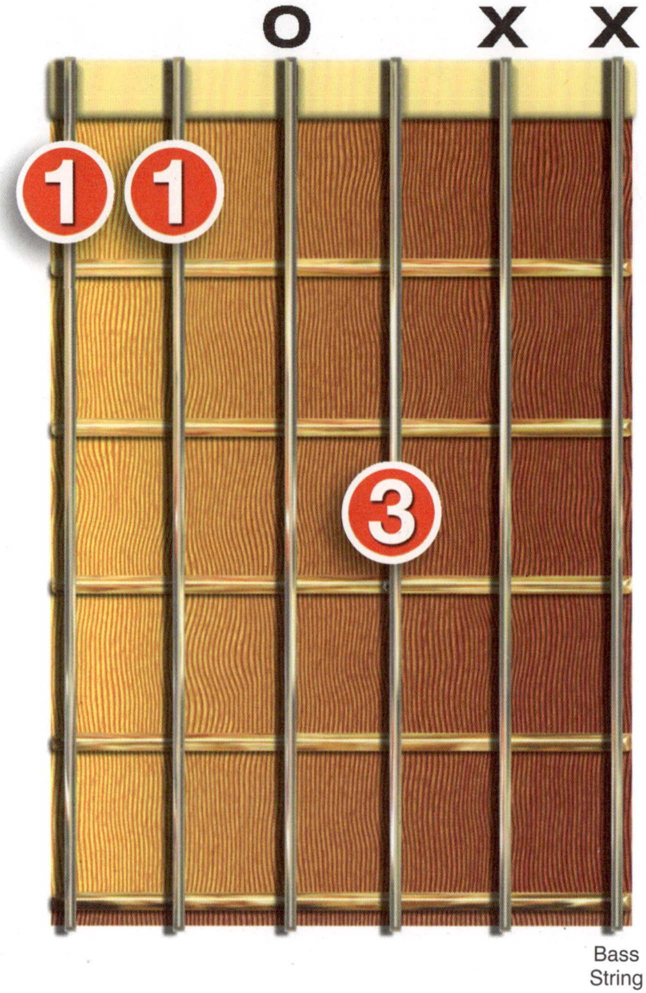

Chord Spelling

1st (F), 2nd (G), 5th (C)

FREE ACCESS on smartphones including iPhone & Android

Using any QR code app scan and **HEAR** the chord

Fsus4

Suspended 4th

Chord Spelling

1st (F), 4th (B♭), 5th (C)

FREE ACCESS on smartphones including iPhone & Android

Using any QR code app scan and **HEAR** the chord

F5

5th (Power Chord)

X X X
1
4
3
Bass String

Chord Spelling

1st (F), 5th (C)

A
A♯/B♭
B
C
C♯/D♭
D
D♯/E♭
E
F
F♯/G♭
G
G♯/A♭

FREE ACCESS on smartphones including iPhone & Android

Using any QR code app scan and **HEAR** the chord

F6

Major 6th

Chord Spelling

1st (F), 3rd (A), 5th (C), 6th (D)

FREE ACCESS on smartphones including iPhone & Android

Using any QR code app scan and **HEAR** the chord

A
A♯/B♭
B
C
C♯/D♭
D
D♯/E♭
E
F
F♯/G♭
G
G♯/A♭

Fm6

Minor 6th

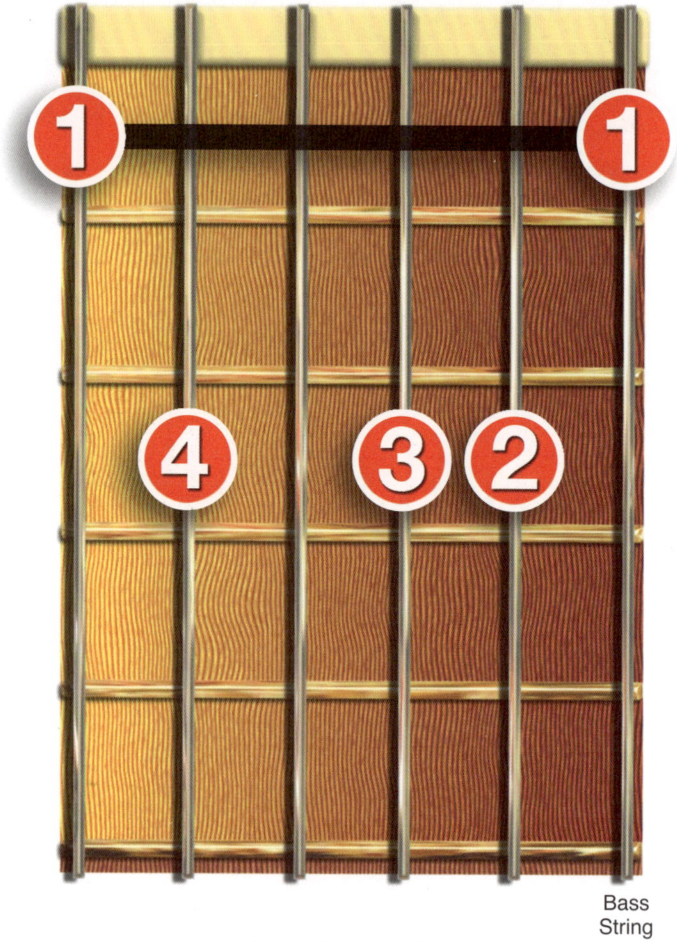

Chord Spelling

1st (F), ♭3rd (A♭), 5th (C), 6th (D)

FREE ACCESS on smartphones including iPhone & Android

Using any QR code app scan and **HEAR** the chord

F6sus4

6th Suspended 4th

Chord Spelling

1st (F), 4th (B♭), 5th (C), 6th (D)

FREE ACCESS on smartphones including iPhone & Android

Using any QR code app scan and **HEAR** the chord

Fmaj7

Major 7th

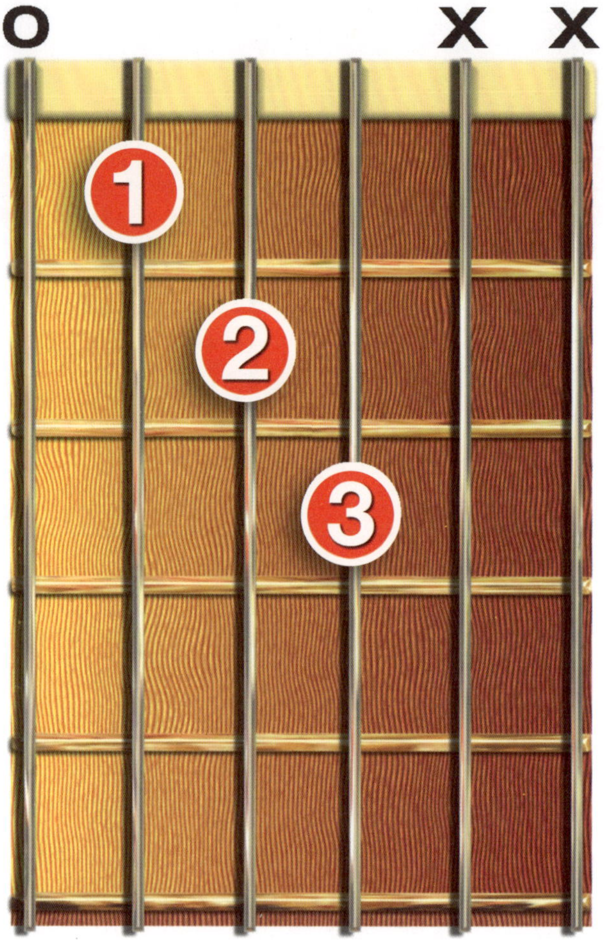

Chord Spelling

1st (F), 3rd (A), 5th (C), 7th (E)

Fm7

Minor 7th

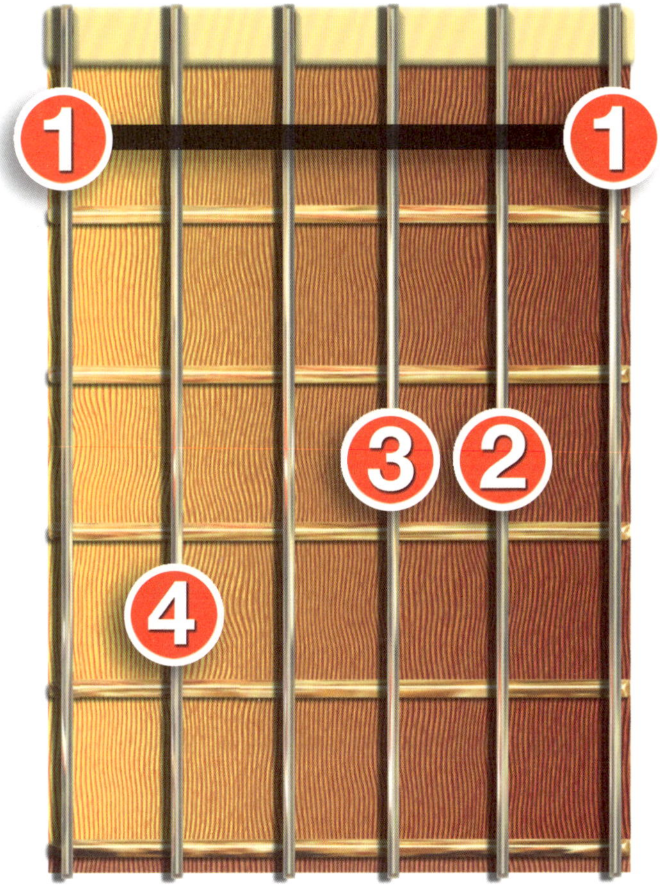

Chord Spelling

1st (F), ♭3rd (A♭), 5th (C), ♭7th (E♭)

FREE ACCESS on smartphones including iPhone & Android

Using any QR code app scan and **HEAR** the chord

F7

Dominant 7th

Bass String

Chord Spelling

1st (F), 3rd (A), 5th (C), ♭7th (E♭)

FREE ACCESS on smartphones including iPhone & Android

Using any QR code app scan and **HEAR** the chord

F°7

Diminished 7th

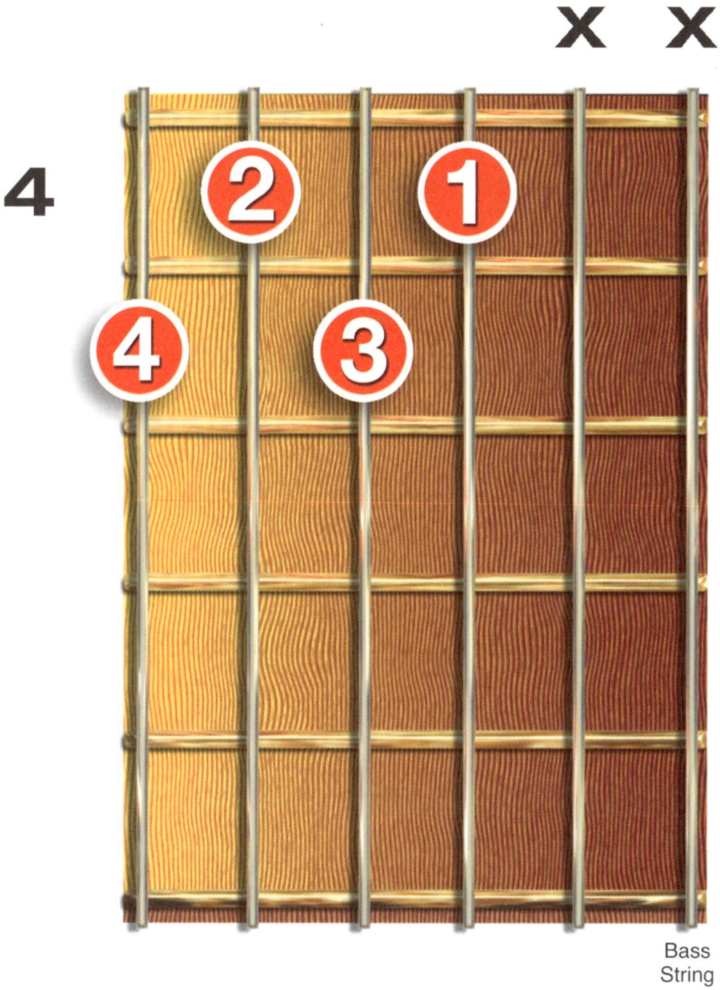

Chord Spelling

1st (F), ♭3rd (A♭), ♭5th (C♭), 𝄫7th (E𝄫)

F7sus4

Dominant 7th Suspended 4th

Chord Spelling

1st (F), 4th (B♭), 5th (C), ♭7th (E♭)

FREE ACCESS on smartphones including iPhone & Android

Using any QR code app scan and **HEAR** the chord

Fmaj9

Major 9th

Chord Spelling

1st (F), 3rd (A), 5th (C), 7th (E), 9th (G)

FREE ACCESS on smartphones including iPhone & Android

Using any QR code app scan and **HEAR** the chord

A
A♯/B♭
B
C
C♯/D♭
D
D♯/E♭
E
F
F♯/G♭
G
G♯/A♭

Fm9

Minor 9th

Chord Spelling

1st (F), ♭3rd (A♭), 5th (C), ♭7th (E♭), 9th (G)

FREE ACCESS on smartphones including iPhone & Android

Using any QR code app scan and **HEAR** the chord

F9

Dominant 9th

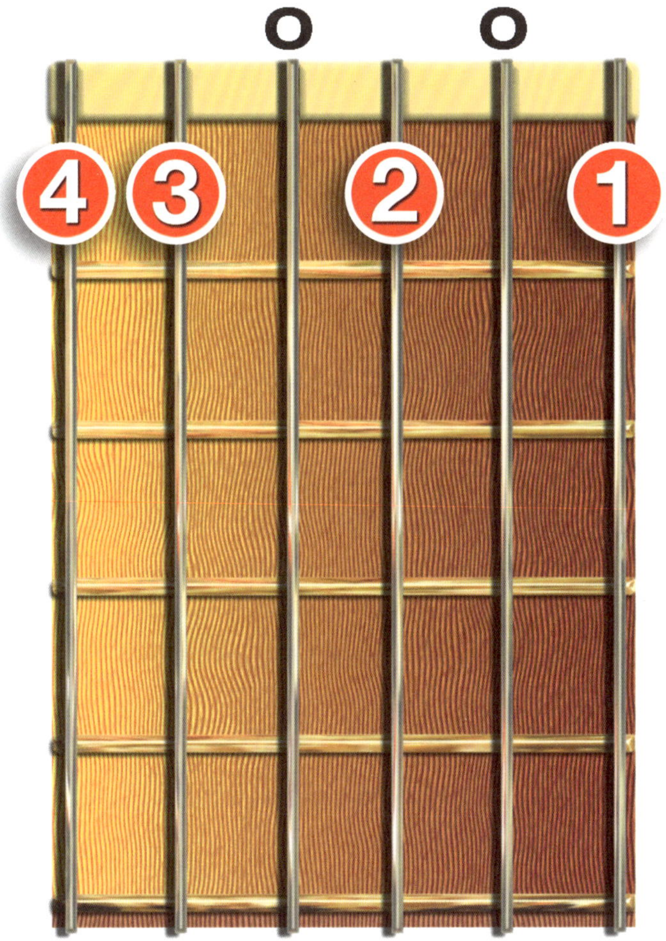

Bass String

Chord Spelling

1st (F), 3rd (A), 5th (C), ♭7th (E♭), 9th (G)

FREE ACCESS on smartphones including iPhone & Android

Using any QR code app scan and **HEAR** the chord

Fmaj11

Major 11th

Chord Spelling

1st (F), 3rd (A), 5th (C), 7th (E), 9th (G), 11th (B♭)

FREE ACCESS on smartphones including iPhone & Android

Using any QR code app scan and **HEAR** the chord

Fmaj13

Major 13th

Chord Spelling

1st (F), 3rd (A), 5th (C), 7th (E), 9th (G), 11th (B♭), 13th (D)

FREE ACCESS on smartphones including iPhone & Android

Using any QR code app scan and **HEAR** the chord

F♯/G♭
Major

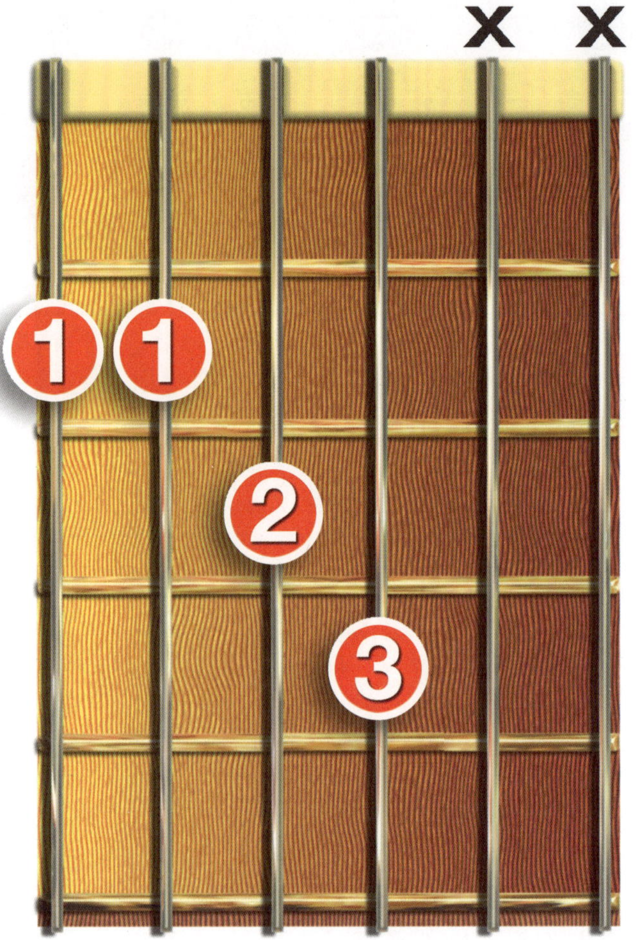

Chord Spelling

1st (F♯), 3rd (A♯), 5th (C♯)

FREE ACCESS on smartphones including iPhone & Android

Using any QR code app scan and **HEAR** the chord

F♯/G♭m
Minor

Chord Spelling

1st (F♯), ♭3rd (A), 5th (C♯)

FREE ACCESS on smartphones including iPhone & Android

Using any QR code app scan and **HEAR** the chord

A
A♯/B♭
B
C
C♯/D♭
D
D♯/E♭
E
F
F♯/G♭
G
G♯/A♭

F♯/G♭+
Augmented Triad

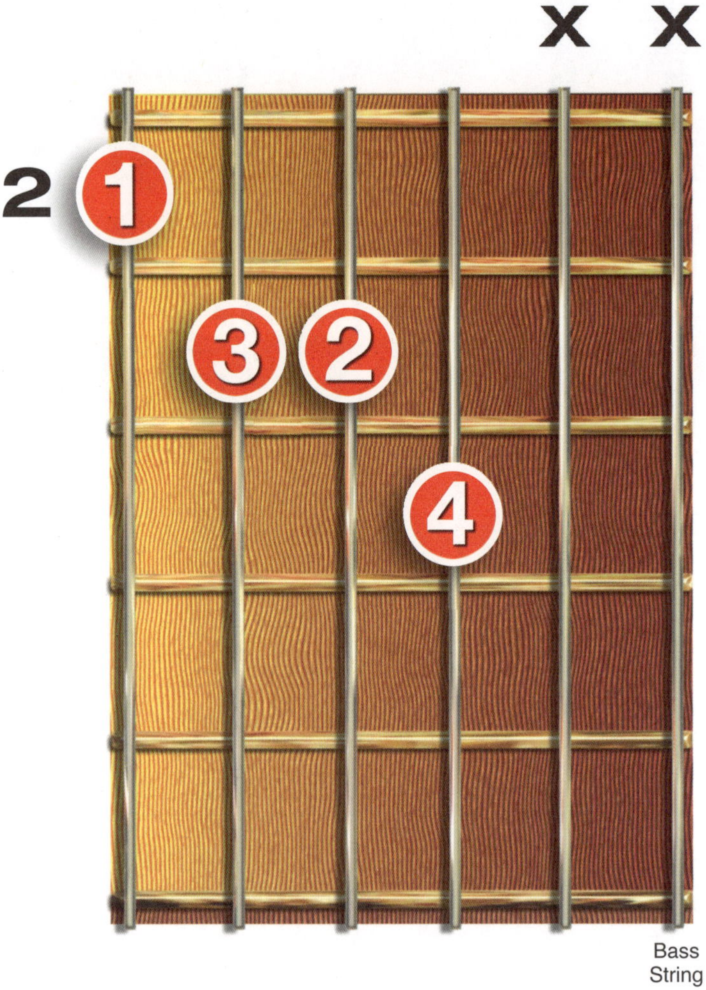
X X
2
1
3
2
4
Bass String

Chord Spelling

1st (F♯), 3rd (A♯), ♯5th (Cx)

FREE ACCESS on smartphones including iPhone & Android

Using any QR code app scan and **HEAR** the chord

F♯/G♭°
Diminished Triad

X X
1
3
2
4
Bass String

Chord Spelling

1st (F♯), ♭3rd (A), ♭5th (C)

FREE ACCESS on smartphones including iPhone & Android

Using any QR code app scan and **HEAR** the chord

A
A♯/B♭
B
C
C♯/D♭
D
D♯/E♭
E
F
F♯/G♭
G
G♯/A♭

F♯/G♭sus2

Suspended 2nd

Chord Spelling

1st (F♯), 2nd (G♯), 5th (A♯)

FREE ACCESS on smartphones including iPhone & Android

Using any QR code app scan and **HEAR** the chord

F♯/G♭sus4
Suspended 4th

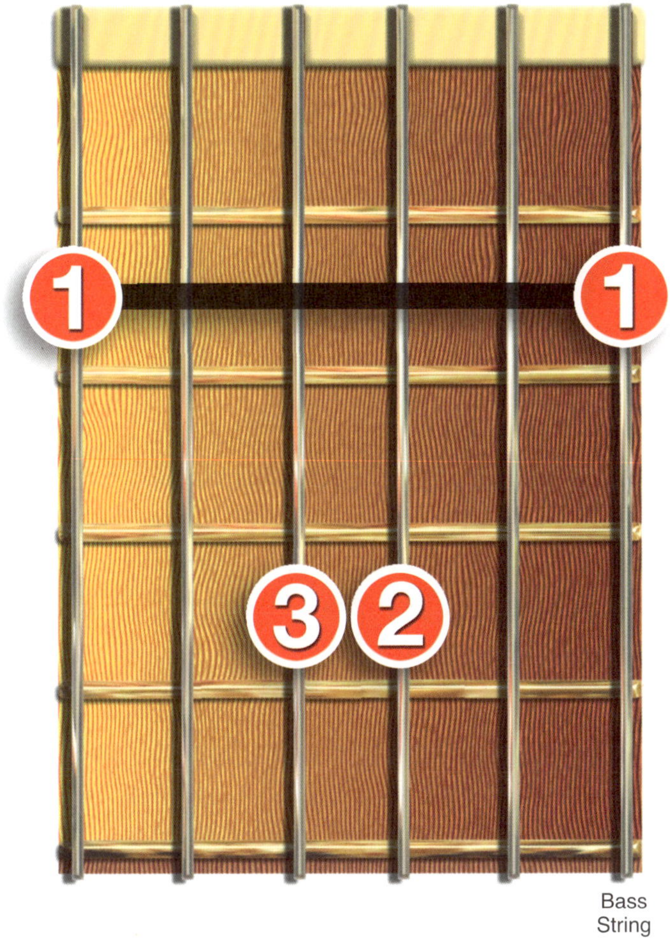

Chord Spelling

1st (F♯), 4th (B), 5th (C♯)

FREE ACCESS on smartphones including iPhone & Android

Using any QR code app scan and **HEAR** the chord

F♯/G♭5

5th (Power Chord)

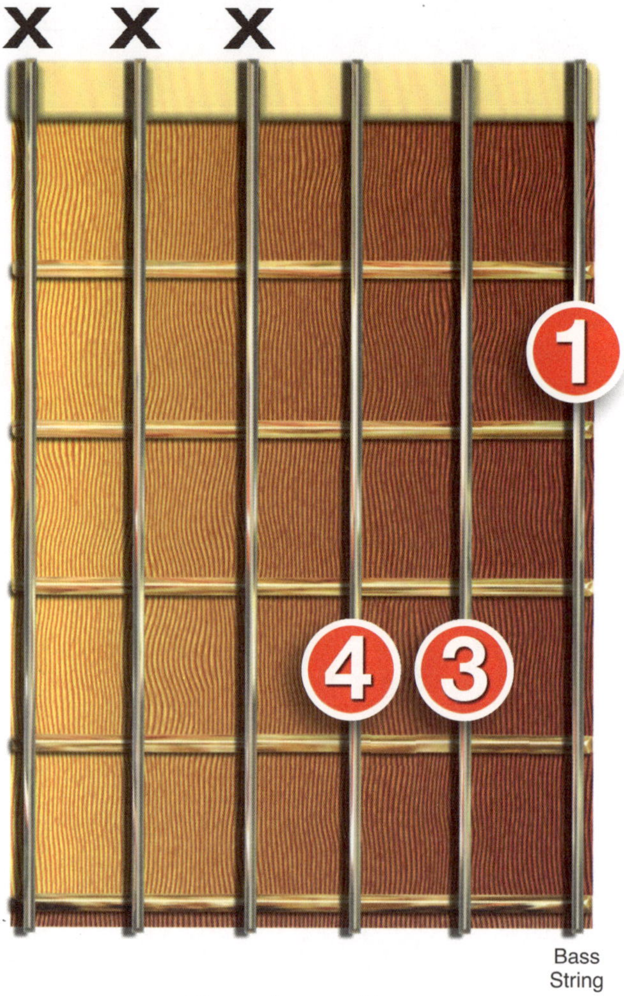

Chord Spelling

1st (F♯), 5th (C♯)

FREE ACCESS on smartphones including iPhone & Android

Using any QR code app scan and **HEAR** the chord

F♯/G♭6

Major 6th

Chord Spelling

1st (F♯), 3rd (A♯), 5th (C♯), 6th (D♯)

FREE ACCESS on smartphones including iPhone & Android

Using any QR code app scan and **HEAR** the chord

A
A♯/B♭
B
C
C♯/D♭
D
D♯/E♭
E
F
F♯/G♭
G
G♯/A♭

A
A♯/B♭
B
C
C♯/D♭
D
D♯/E♭
E
F
F♯/G♭
G
G♯/A♭

F♯/G♭m6

Minor 6th

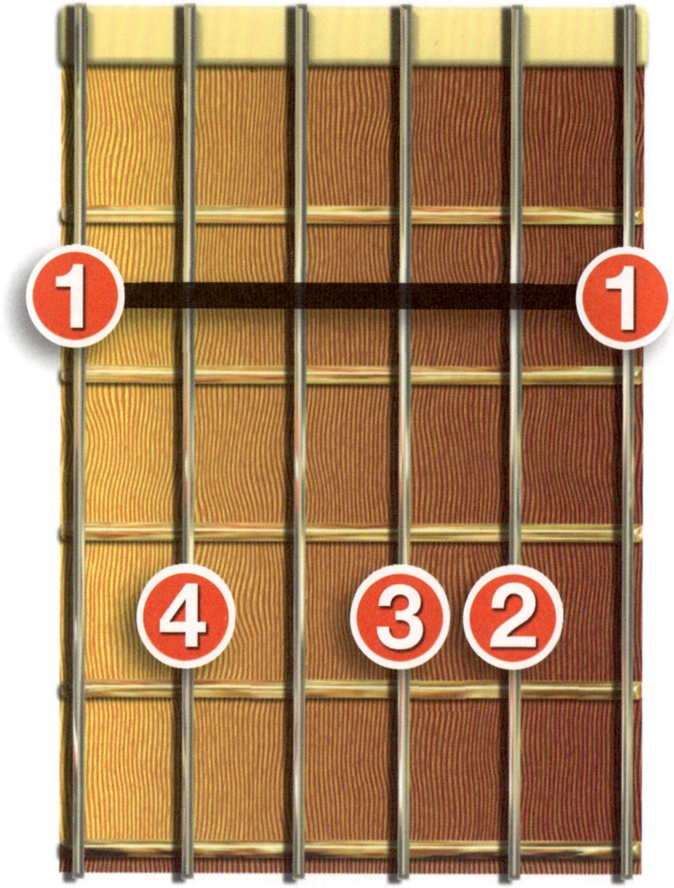

Chord Spelling

1st (F♯), ♭3rd (A), 5th (C♯), 6th (D♯)

FREE ACCESS on smartphones including iPhone & Android

Using any QR code app scan and **HEAR** the chord

F♯/G♭6sus4

6th Suspended 4th

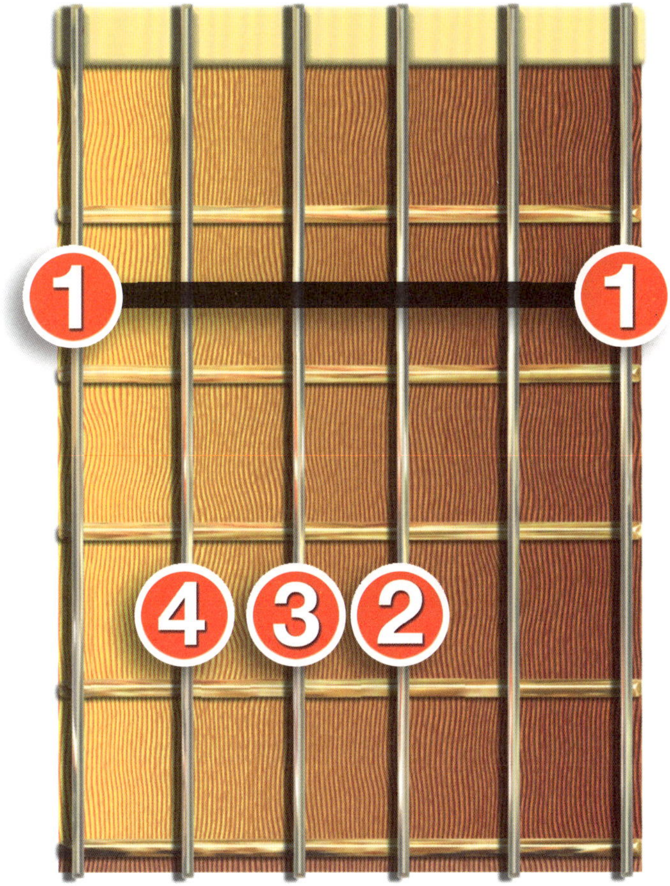

Chord Spelling

1st (F♯), 4th (B), 5th (C♯), 6th (D♯)

FREE ACCESS on smartphones including iPhone & Android

Using any QR code app scan and **HEAR** the chord

A
A♯/B♭
B
C
C♯/D♭
D
D♯/E♭
E
F
F♯/G♭
G
G♯/A♭

F♯/G♭maj7

Major 7th

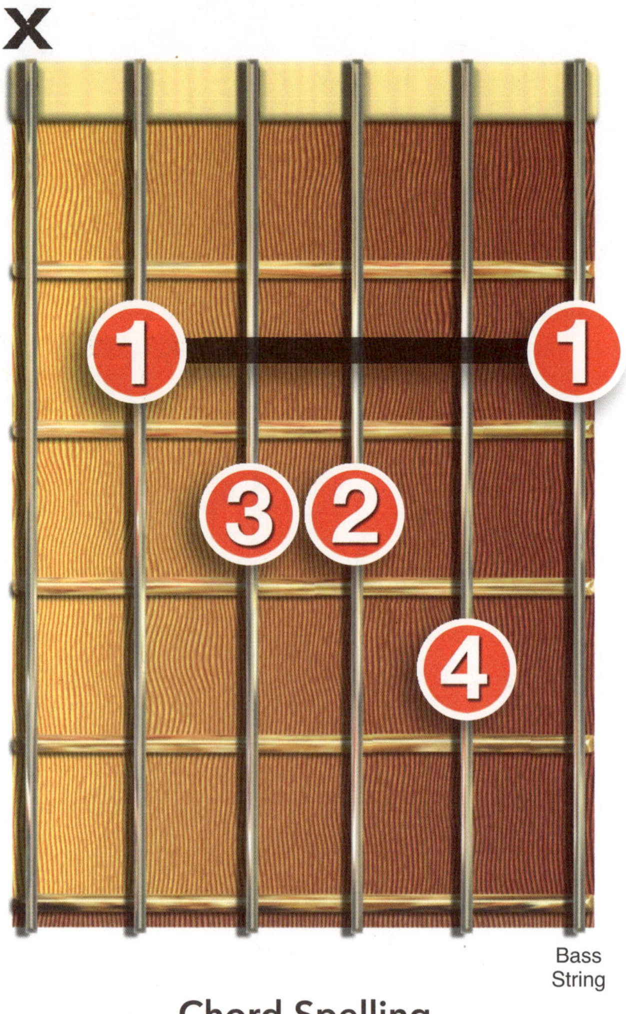

Chord Spelling

1st (F♯), 3rd (A♯), 5th (C♯), 7th (F)

FREE ACCESS on smartphones including iPhone & Android

Using any QR code app scan and **HEAR** the chord

F♯/G♭m7
Minor 7th

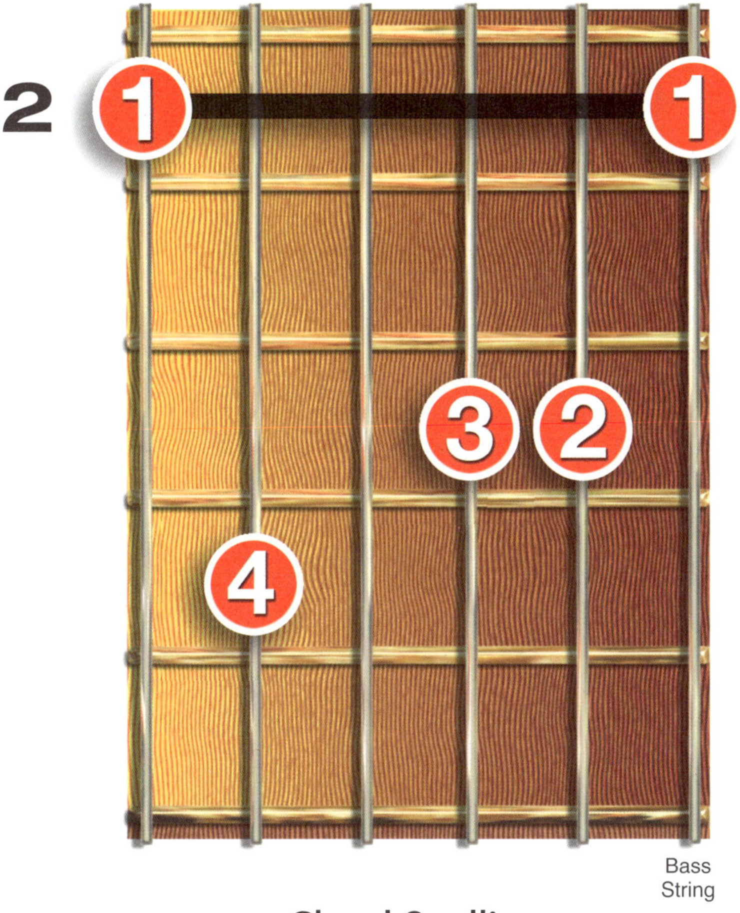

Chord Spelling

1st (F♯), ♭3rd (A), 5th (C♯), ♭7th (E)

FREE ACCESS on smartphones including iPhone & Android

Using any QR code app scan and **HEAR** the chord

A
A♯/B♭
B
C
C♯/D♭
D
D♯/E♭
E
F
F♯/G♭
G
G♯/A♭

A
A♯/B♭
B
C
C♯/D♭
D
D♯/E♭
E
F
F♯/G♭
G
G♯/A♭

F♯/G♭7
Dominant 7th

Chord Spelling

1st (F♯), 3rd (A♯), 5th (C♯), ♭7th (E)

F♯/G♭°7
Diminished 7th

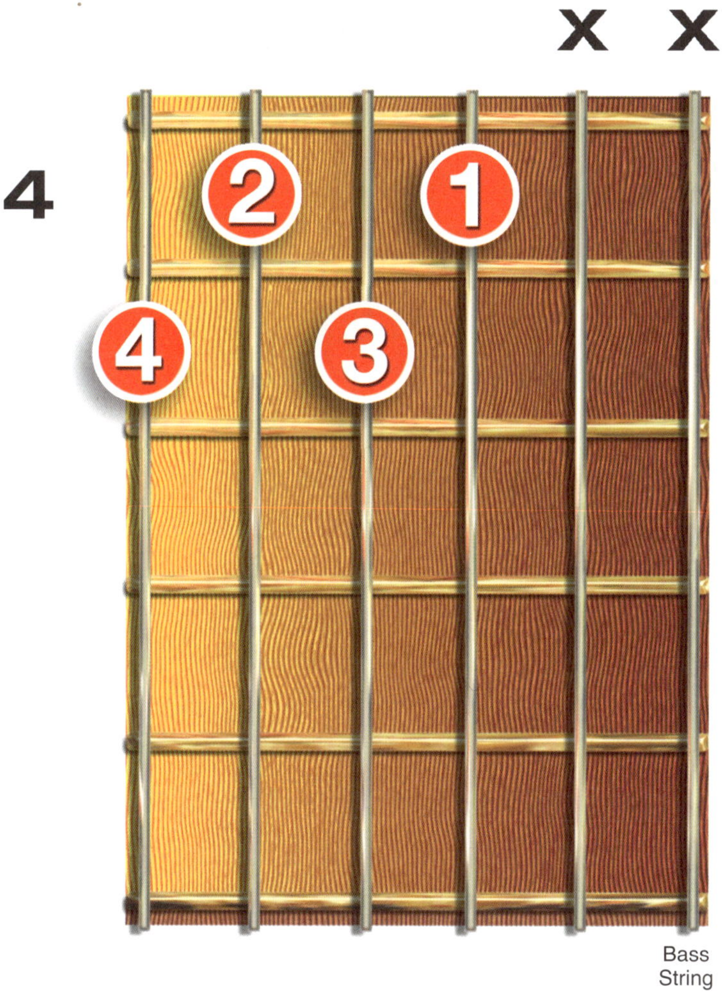

X X
4
2
1
4
3
Bass String

Chord Spelling

1st (F♯), ♭3rd (A), ♭5th (C), ♭♭7th (E♭)

FREE ACCESS on smartphones including iPhone & Android

Using any QR code app scan and **HEAR** the chord

F♯/G♭7sus4

Dominant 7th Suspended 4th

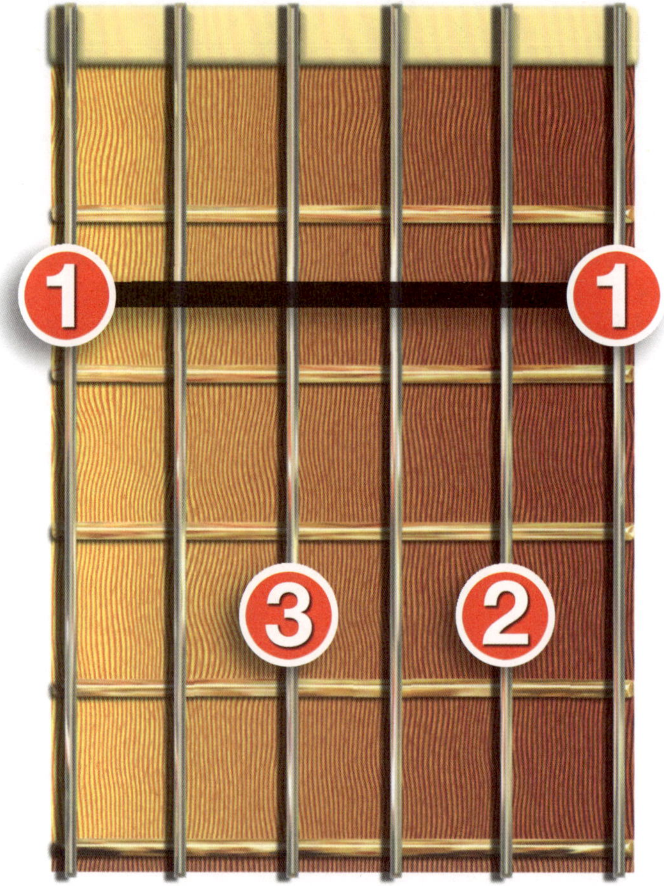

Chord Spelling

1st (F♯), 4th (B), 5th (C♯), ♭7th (E)

FREE ACCESS on smartphones including iPhone & Android

Using any QR code app scan and **HEAR** the chord

F♯/G♭maj9
Major 9th

Chord Spelling

1st (F♯), 3rd (A♯), 5th (C♯), 7th (E♯), 9th (G♯)

FREE ACCESS on smartphones including iPhone & Android

Using any QR code app scan and **HEAR** the chord

F♯/G♭m9

Minor 9th

Chord Spelling

1st (F♯), ♭3rd (A), 5th (C♯), ♭7th (E), 9th (G♯)

FREE ACCESS on smartphones including iPhone & Android

Using any QR code app scan and **HEAR** the chord

F♯/G♭9
Dominant 9th

Chord Spelling

1st (F♯), 3rd (A♯), 5th (C♯), ♭7th (E), 9th (G♯)

FREE ACCESS on smartphones including iPhone & Android

Using any QR code app scan and **HEAR** the chord

F♯/G♭maj11

Major 11th

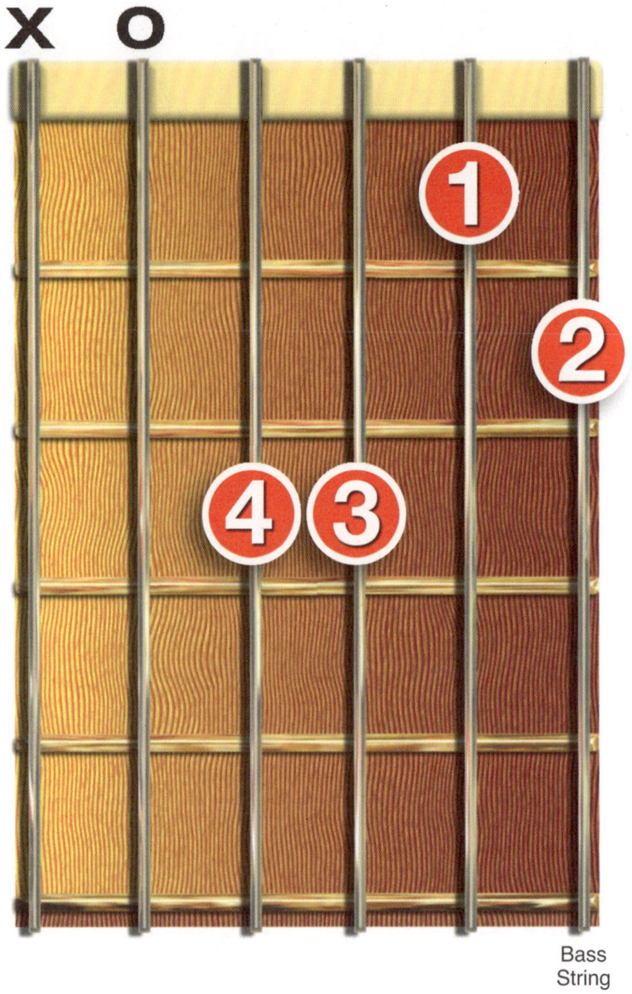

Chord Spelling

1st (F♯), 3rd (A♯), 5th (C♯), 7th (E♯), 9th (G♯), 11th (B)

FREE ACCESS on smartphones including iPhone & Android

Using any QR code app scan and **HEAR** the chord

F♯/G♭maj13

Major 13th

Chord Spelling

1st (F♯), 3rd (A♯), 5th (C♯), 7th (E♯), 9th (G♯), 11th (B), 13th (D♯)

FREE ACCESS on smartphones including iPhone & Android

Using any QR code app scan and **HEAR** the chord

G

Major

Chord Spelling

1st (G), 3rd (B), 5th (D)

FREE ACCESS on smartphones including iPhone & Android

Using any QR code app scan and **HEAR** the chord

Gm

Minor

Chord Spelling

1st (G), ♭3rd (B♭), 5th (D)

A
A♯/B♭
B
C
C♯/D♭
D
D♯/E♭
E
F
F♯/G♭
G
G♯/A♭

G+

Augmented Triad

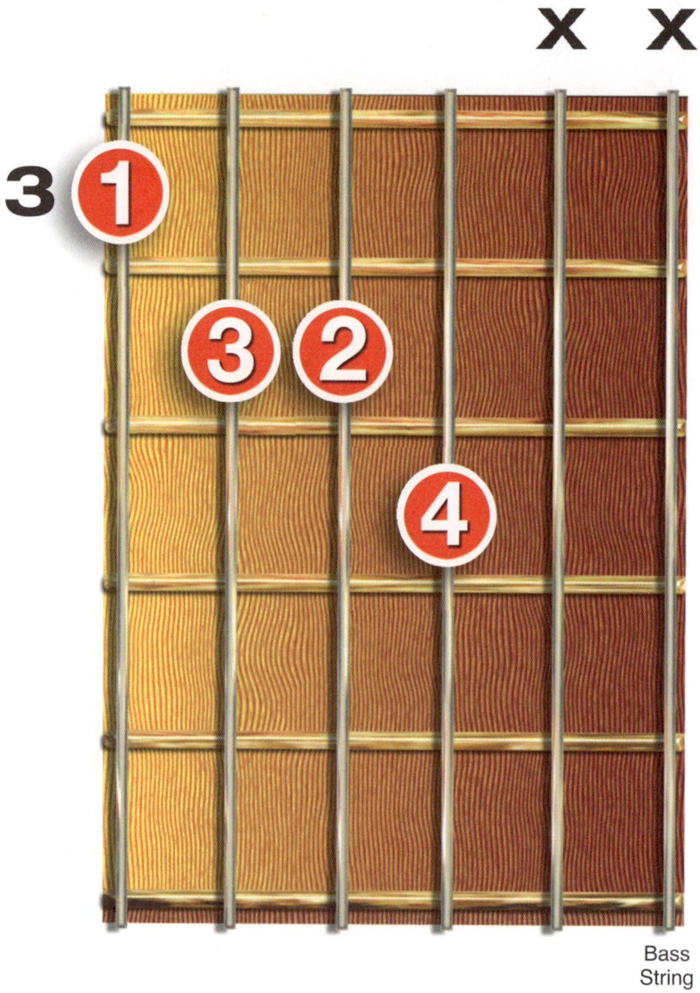

Chord Spelling

1st (G), 3rd (B), ♯5th (D♯)

FREE ACCESS on smartphones including iPhone & Android

Using any QR code app scan and **HEAR** the chord

G°

Diminished Triad

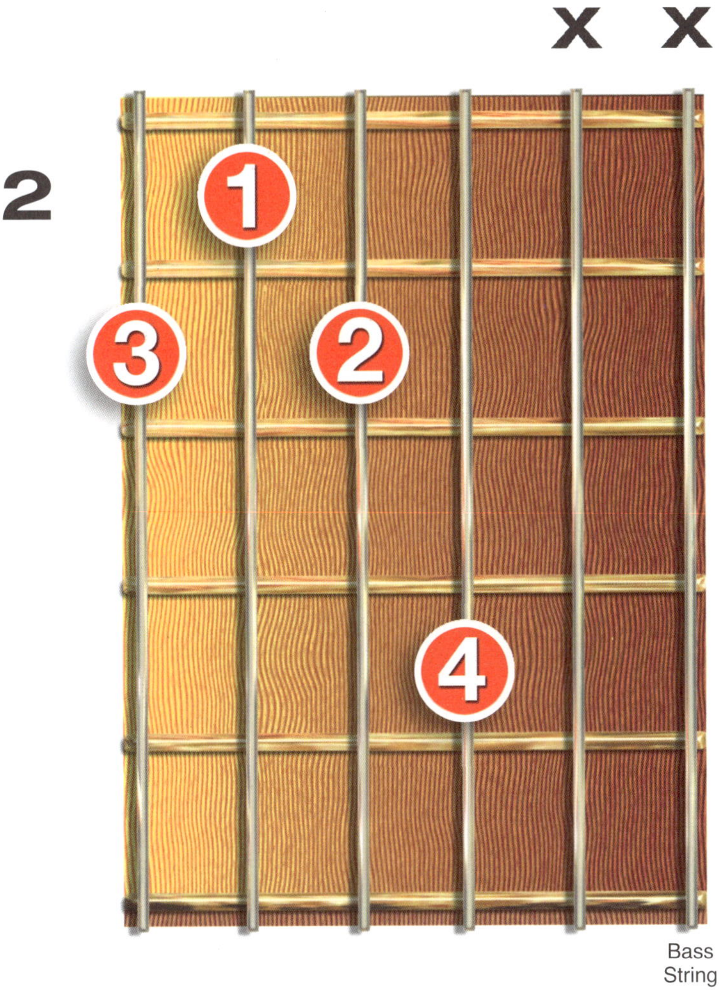

Chord Spelling

1st (G), ♭3rd (B♭), ♭5th (D♭)

FREE ACCESS on smartphones including iPhone & Android

Using any QR code app scan and **HEAR** the chord

Gsus2

Suspended 2nd

Chord Spelling

1st (G), 2nd (A), 5th (D)

FREE ACCESS on smartphones including iPhone & Android

Using any QR code app scan and **HEAR** the chord

Gsus4

Suspended 4th

O O X
1
4
3
Bass
String

Chord Spelling

1st (G), 4th (C), 5th (D)

FREE ACCESS on smartphones including iPhone & Android

Using any QR code app scan and **HEAR** the chord

G5

5th (Power Chord)

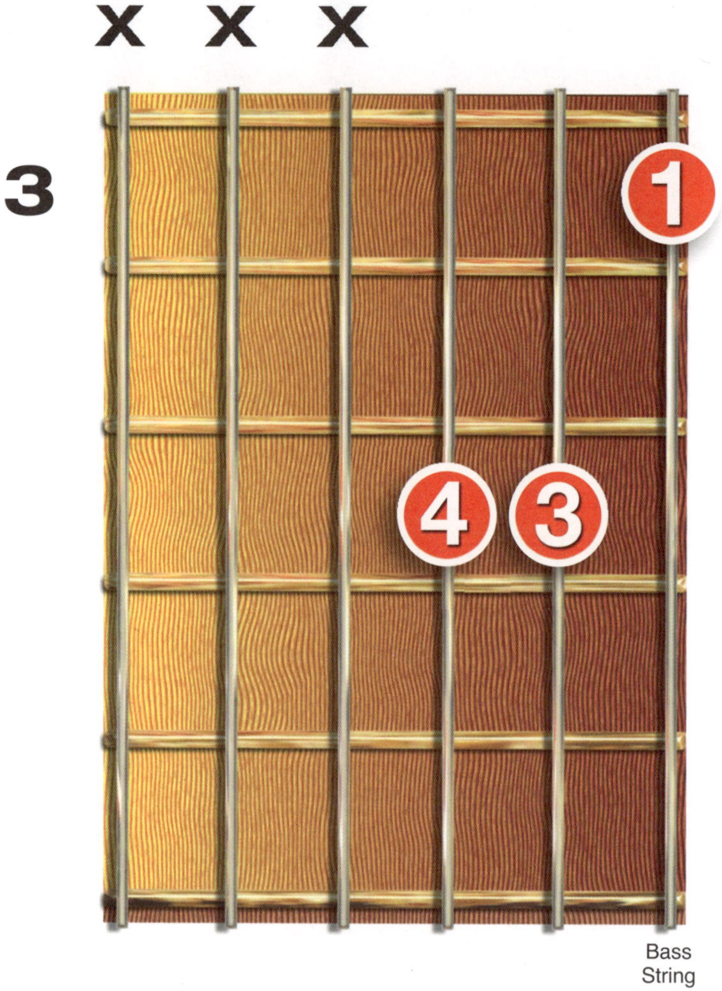
X X X
3
1
4 3
Bass String

Chord Spelling

1st (G), 5th (D)

G6

Major 6th

Chord Spelling

1st (G), 3rd (B), 5th (D), 6th (E)

FREE ACCESS on smartphones including iPhone & Android

Using any QR code app scan and **HEAR** the chord

A
A♯/B♭
B
C
C♯/D♭
D
D♯/E♭
E
F
F♯/G♭
G
G♯/A♭

Gm6

Minor 6th

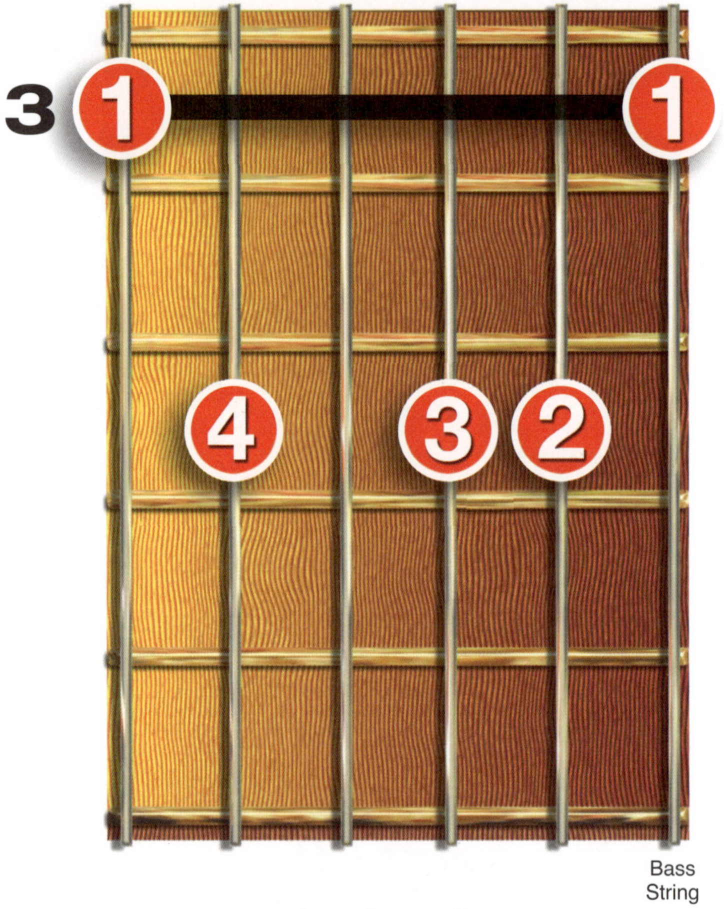

Chord Spelling

1st (G), ♭3rd (B♭), 5th (D), 6th (E)

G6sus4

6th Suspended 4th

Bass String

Chord Spelling

1st (G), 4th (C), 5th (D), 6th (E)

FREE ACCESS on smartphones including iPhone & Android

Using any QR code app scan and **HEAR** the chord

Gmaj7

Major 7th

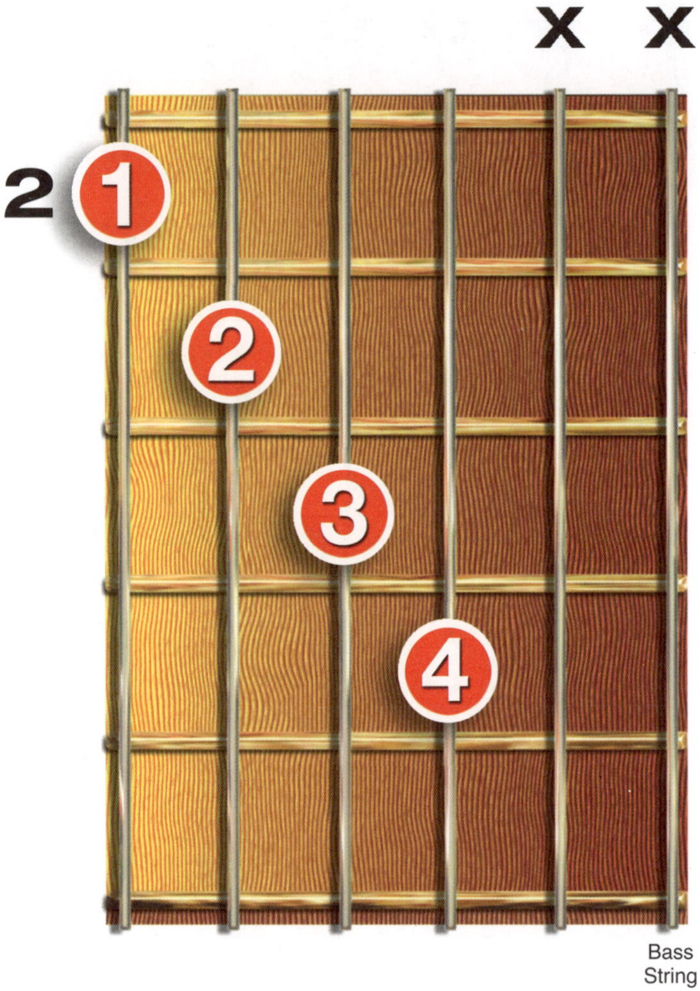

Chord Spelling

1st (G), 3rd (B), 5th (D), 7th (F♯)

FREE ACCESS on smartphones including iPhone & Android

Using any QR code app scan and **HEAR** the chord

Gm7

Minor 7th

Chord Spelling

1st (G), ♭3rd (B♭), 5th (D), ♭7th (F)

FREE ACCESS on smartphones including iPhone & Android

Using any QR code app scan and **HEAR** the chord

G7

Dominant 7th

Bass String

Chord Spelling

1st (G), 3rd (B), 5th (D), ♭7th (F)

FREE ACCESS on smartphones including iPhone & Android

Using any QR code app scan and **HEAR** the chord

G°7

Diminished 7th

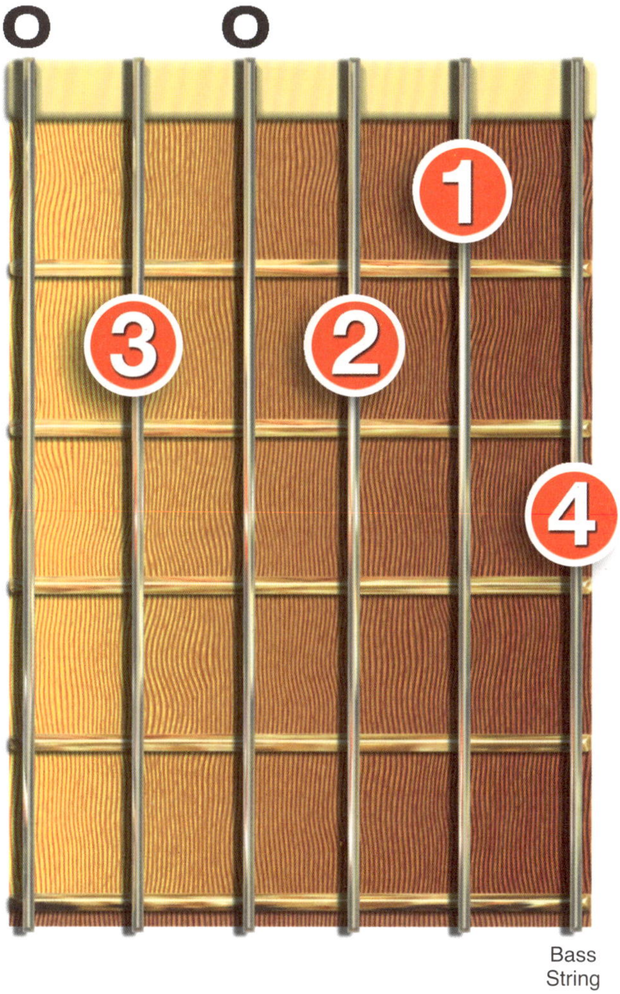

Chord Spelling

1st (G), ♭3rd (B♭), ♭5th (D♭), 𝄫7th (F♭)

FREE ACCESS on smartphones including iPhone & Android

Using any QR code app scan and **HEAR** the chord

G7sus4

Dominant 7th Suspended 4th

Chord Spelling

1st (G), 4th (C), 5th (D), ♭7th (F)

FREE ACCESS on smartphones including iPhone & Android

Using any QR code app scan and **HEAR** the chord

Gmaj9
Major 9th

Chord Spelling

1st (G), 3rd (B), 5th (D), 7th (F♯), 9th (A)

FREE ACCESS on smartphones including iPhone & Android

Using any QR code app scan and **HEAR** the chord

Gm9

Minor 9th

Chord Spelling

1st (G), ♭3rd (B♭), 5th (D), ♭7th (F), 9th (A)

FREE ACCESS on smartphones including iPhone & Android

Using any QR code app scan and **HEAR** the chord

G9

Dominant 9th

Chord Spelling

1st (G), 3rd (B), 5th (D), ♭7th (F), 9th (A)

FREE ACCESS on smartphones including iPhone & Android

Using any QR code app scan and **HEAR** the chord

Gmaj11

Major 11th

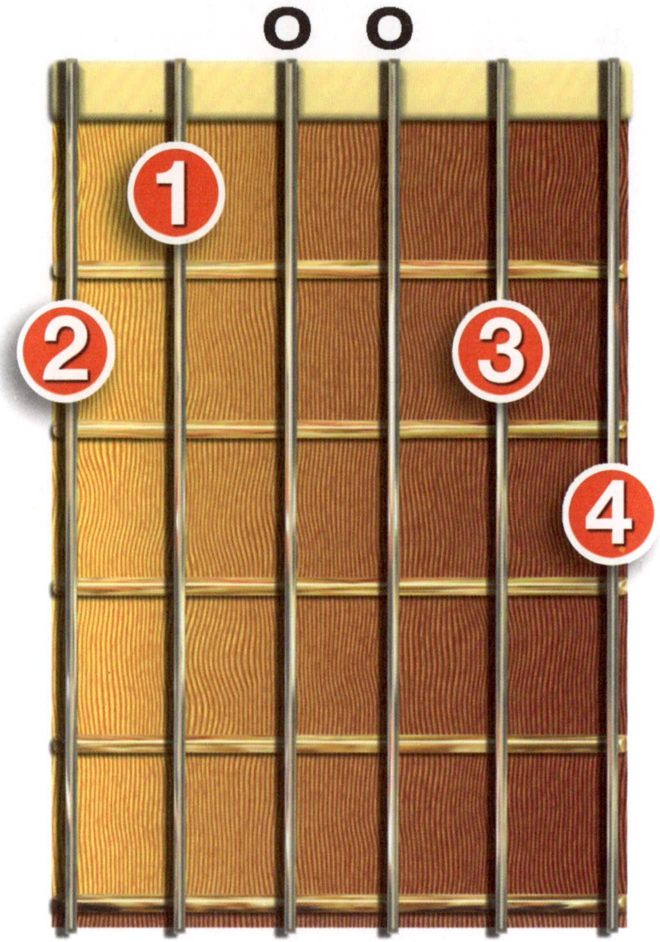

Chord Spelling

1st (G), 3rd (B), 5th (D), 7th (F♯), 9th (A), 11th (C)

FREE ACCESS on smartphones including iPhone & Android

Using any QR code app scan and **HEAR** the chord

Gmaj13
Major 13th

Chord Spelling

1st (G), 3rd (B), 5th (D), 7th (F♯), 9th (A), 11th (C), 13th (E)

FREE ACCESS on smartphones including iPhone & Android

Using any QR code app scan and **HEAR** the chord

G#/Ab
Major

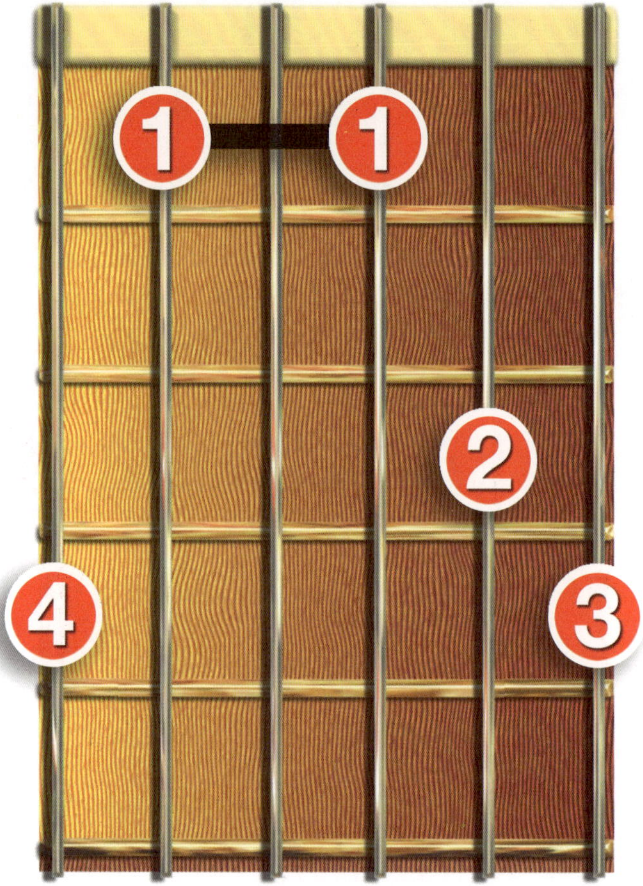
1
1
2
4
3
Bass
String

Chord Spelling

1st (Ab), 3rd (C), 5th (Eb)

FREE ACCESS on smartphones including iPhone & Android

Using any QR code app scan and **HEAR** the chord

G♯/A♭m
Minor

4
1
1
4
3
Bass String

Chord Spelling

1st (A♭), ♭3rd (C♭), 5th (E♭)

G♯/A♭+
Augmented Triad

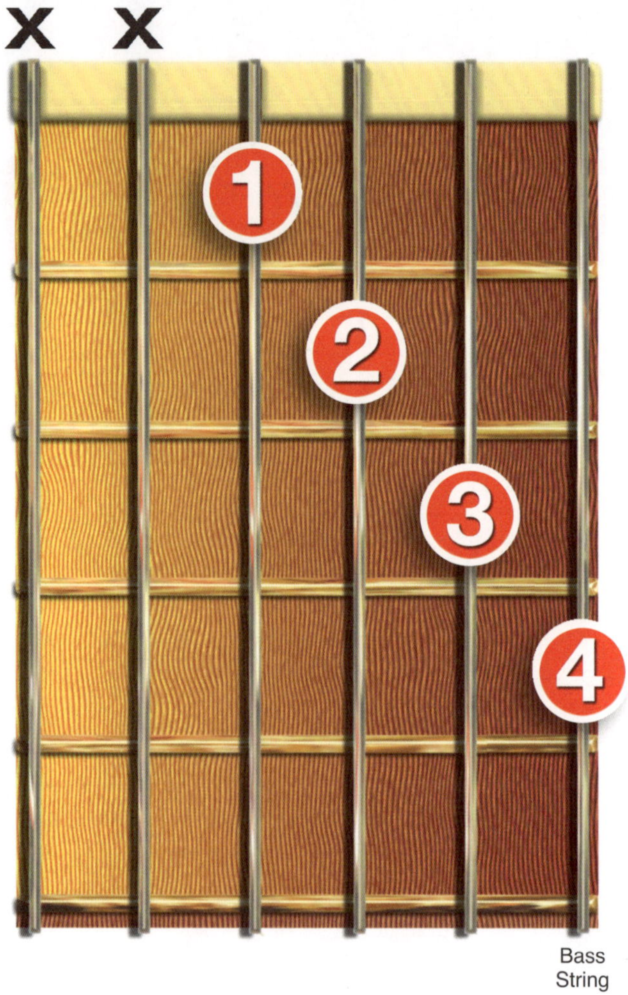

Chord Spelling

1st (A♭), 3rd (C), ♯5th (E)

FREE ACCESS on smartphones including iPhone & Android

Using any QR code app scan and **HEAR** the chord

G♯/A♭°
Diminished Triad

Chord Spelling

1st (A♭), ♭3rd (C♭), ♭5th (E♭♭)

FREE ACCESS on smartphones including iPhone & Android

Using any QR code app scan and **HEAR** the chord

G♯/A♭sus2
Suspended 2nd

Chord Spelling

1st (A♭), 2nd (B♭), 5th (E♭)

FREE ACCESS on smartphones including iPhone & Android

Using any QR code app scan and **HEAR** the chord

G♯/A♭sus4

Suspended 4th

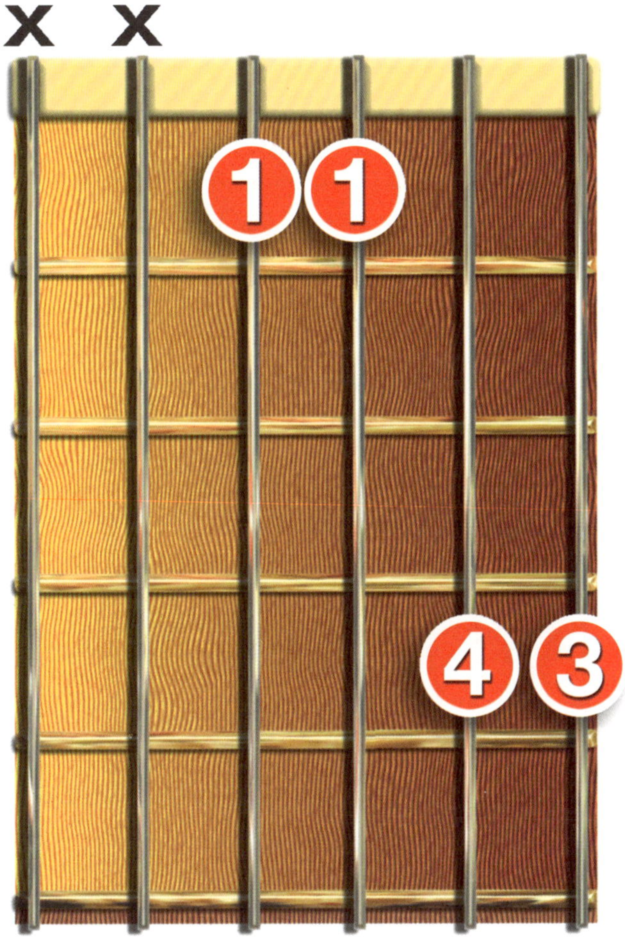

Bass String

Chord Spelling

1st (A♭), 4th (D♭), 5th (E♭)

FREE ACCESS on smartphones including iPhone & Android

Using any QR code app scan and **HEAR** the chord

G♯/A♭5

5th (Power Chord)

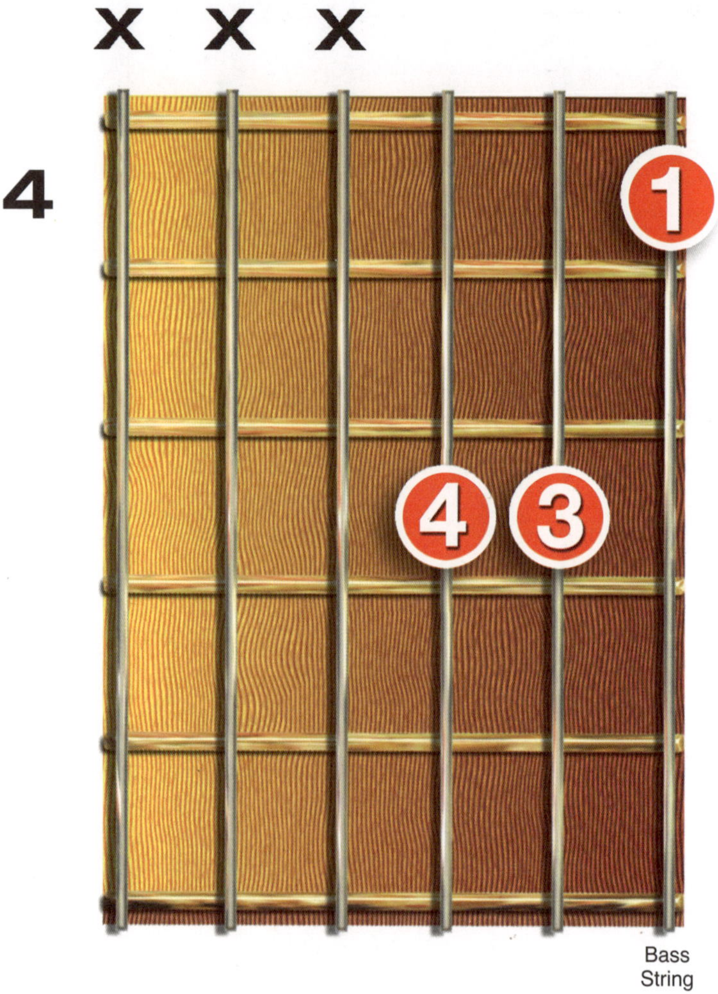

Chord Spelling

1st (A♭), 5th (E♭)

FREE ACCESS on smartphones including iPhone & Android

Using any QR code app scan and **HEAR** the chord

G♯/A♭6
Major 6th

Chord Spelling

1st (A♭), 3rd (C), 5th (E♭), 6th (F)

FREE ACCESS on smartphones including iPhone & Android

Using any QR code app scan and **HEAR** the chord

A
A♯/B♭
B
C
C♯/D♭
D
D♯/E♭
E
F
F♯/G♭
G
G♯/A♭

G♯/A♭m6

Minor 6th

Chord Spelling

1st (A♭), ♭3rd (C♭), 5th (E♭), 6th (F)

FREE ACCESS on smartphones including iPhone & Android

Using any QR code app scan and **HEAR** the chord

G♯/A♭6sus4

6th Suspended 4th

Chord Spelling

1st (A♭), 4th (D♭), 5th (E♭), 6th (F)

FREE ACCESS on smartphones including iPhone & Android

Using any QR code app scan and **HEAR** the chord

A
A♯/B♭
B
C
C♯/D♭
D
D♯/E♭
E
F
F♯/G♭
G
G♯/A♭

G♯/A♭maj7

Major 7th

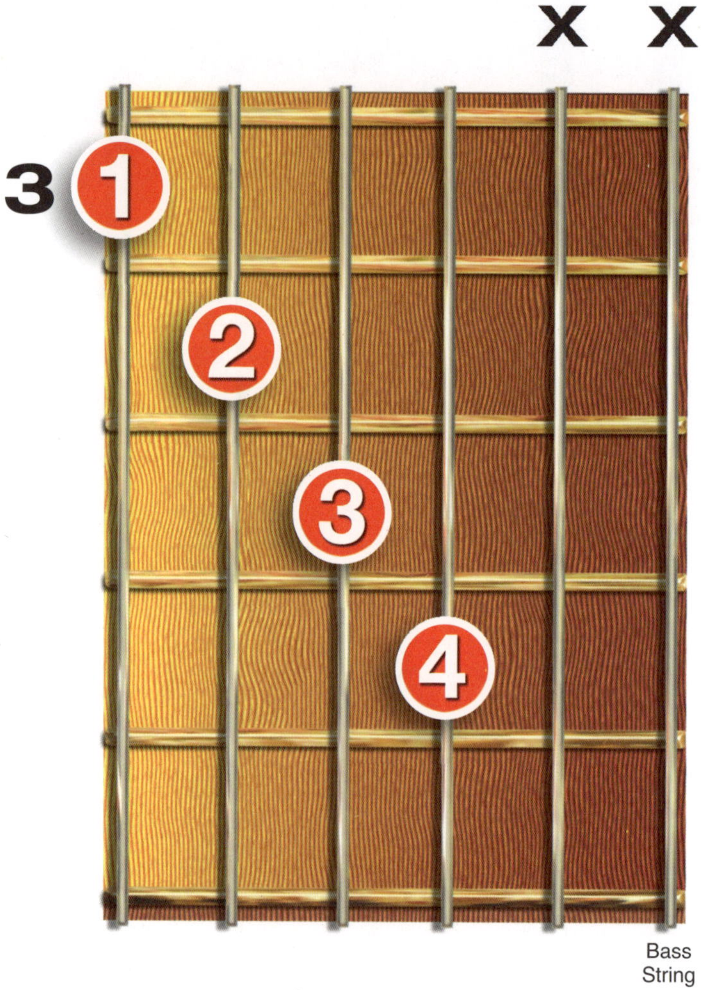
X X
3
1
2
3
4
Bass String

Chord Spelling

1st (A♭), 3rd (C), 5th (E♭), 7th (G)

FREE ACCESS on smartphones including iPhone & Android

Using any QR code app scan and **HEAR** the chord

G♯/A♭m7

Minor 7th

Chord Spelling

1st (A♭), ♭3rd (C♭), 5th (E♭), ♭7th (G♭)

FREE ACCESS on smartphones including iPhone & Android

Using any QR code app scan and **HEAR** the chord

2 G♯/A♭7

Dominant 7th

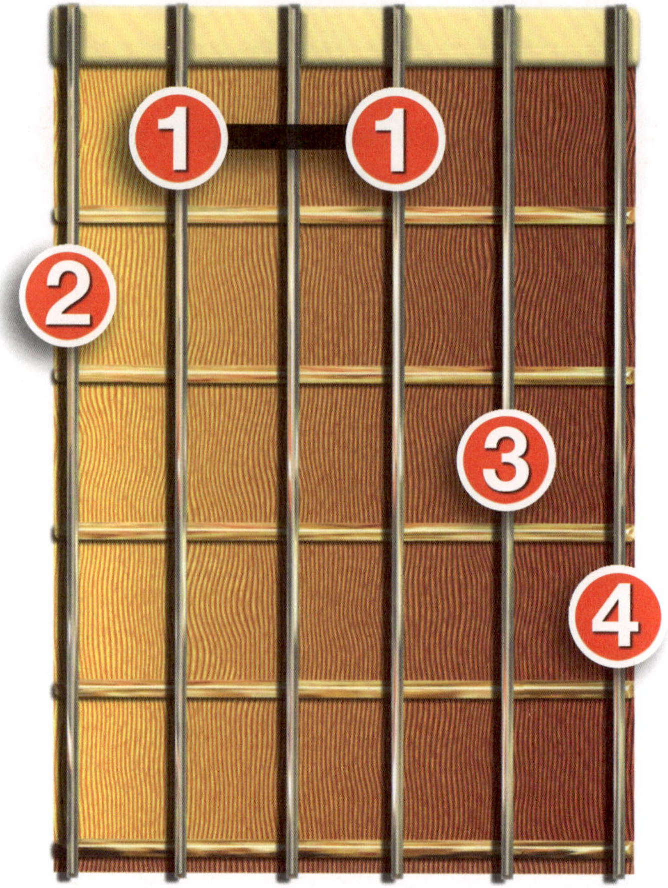

Chord Spelling

1st (A♭), 3rd (C), 5th (E♭), ♭7th (G♭)

FREE ACCESS on smartphones including iPhone & Android

Using any QR code app scan and **HEAR** the chord

G♯/A♭°7

Diminished 7th

Chord Spelling

1st (A♭), ♭3rd (C♭), ♭5th (E♭♭), ♭♭7th (G♭♭)

FREE ACCESS on smartphones including iPhone & Android

Using any QR code app scan and **HEAR** the chord

G♯/A♭7sus4

Dominant 7th Suspended 4th

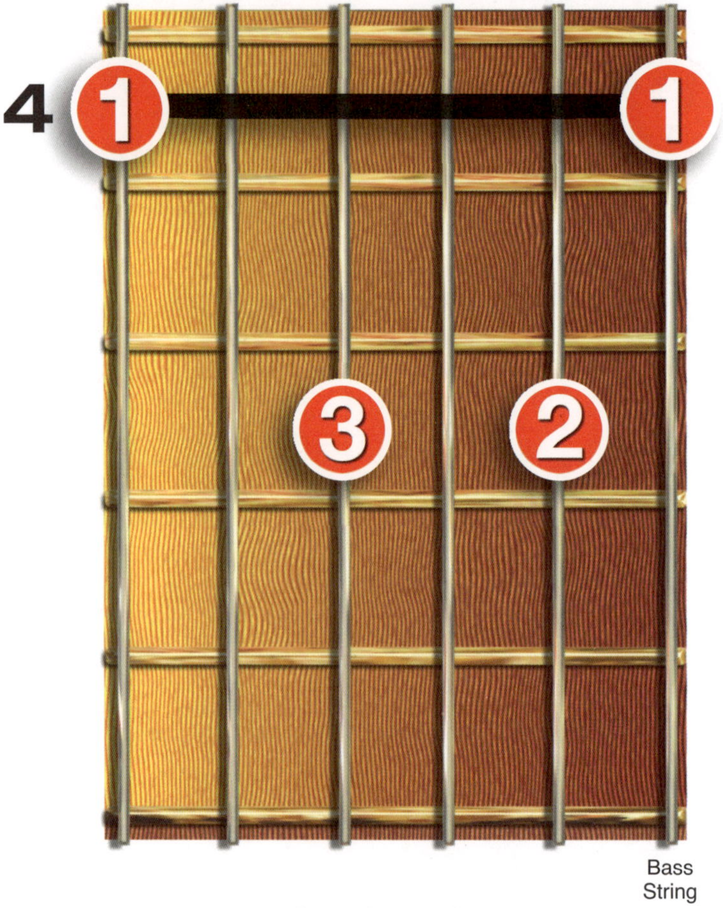

Chord Spelling

1st (A♭), 4th (D♭), 5th (E♭), ♭7th (G♭)

FREE ACCESS on smartphones including iPhone & Android

Using any QR code app scan and **HEAR** the chord

G♯/A♭maj9
Major 9th

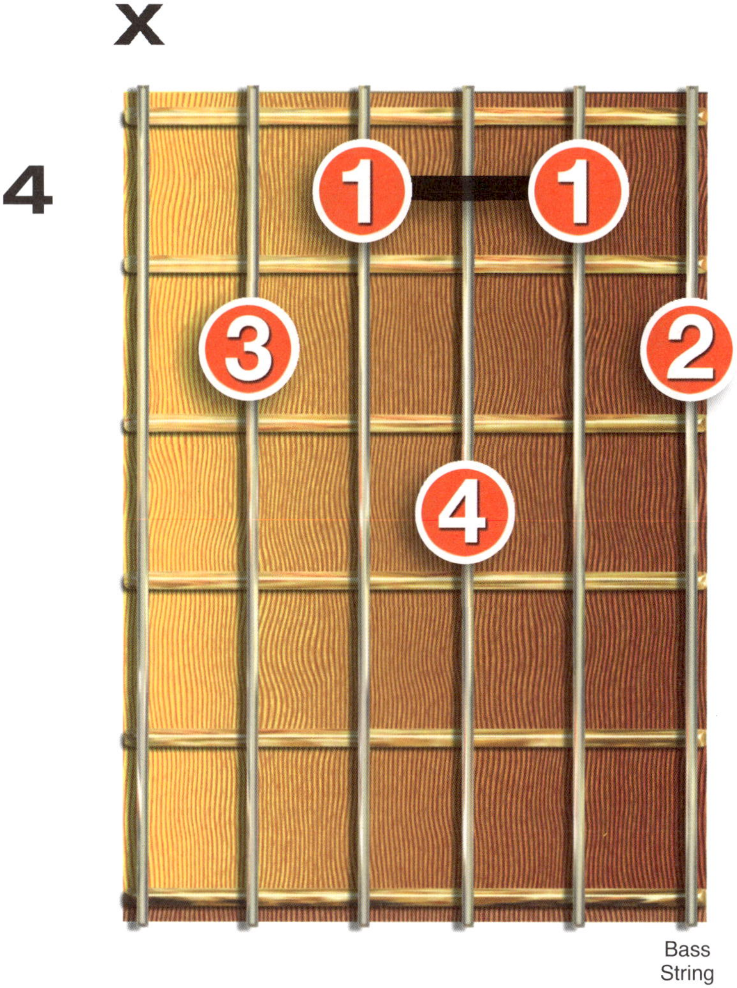

Chord Spelling

1st (A♭), 3rd (C), 5th (E♭), 7th (G), 9th (B♭)

FREE ACCESS on smartphones including iPhone & Android

Using any QR code app scan and **HEAR** the chord

G♯/A♭m9

Minor 9th

A
A♯/B♭
B
C
C♯/D♭
D
D♯/E♭
E
F
F♯/G♭
G
G♯/A♭

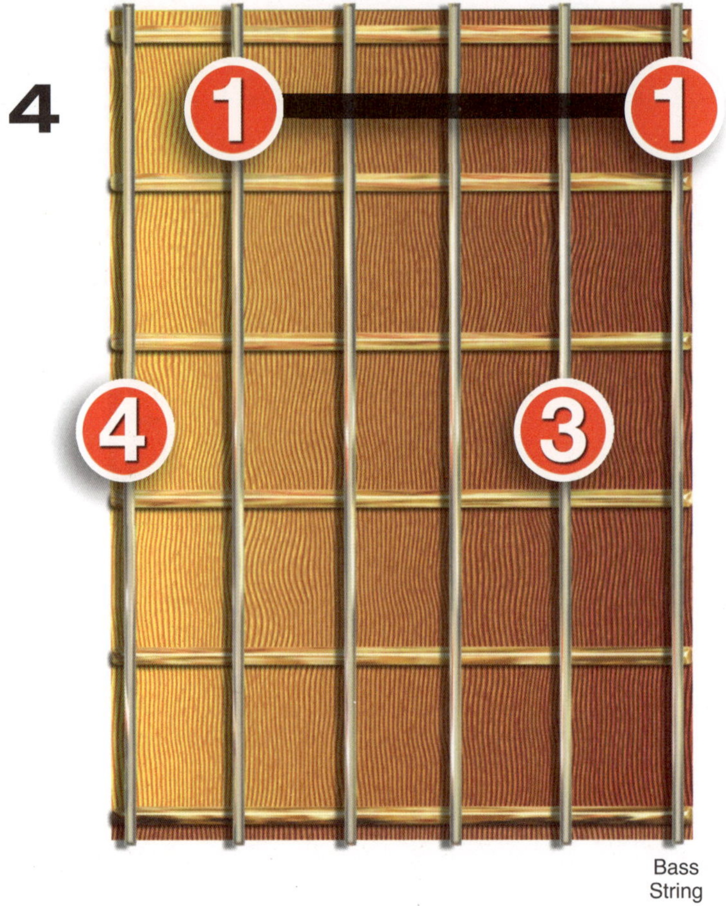
4
1
1
4
3
Bass String

Chord Spelling

1st (A♭), ♭3rd (C♭), 5th (E♭), ♭7th (G♭), 9th (B♭)

FREE ACCESS on smartphones including iPhone & Android

Using any QR code app scan and **HEAR** the chord

G♯/A♭9

Dominant 9th

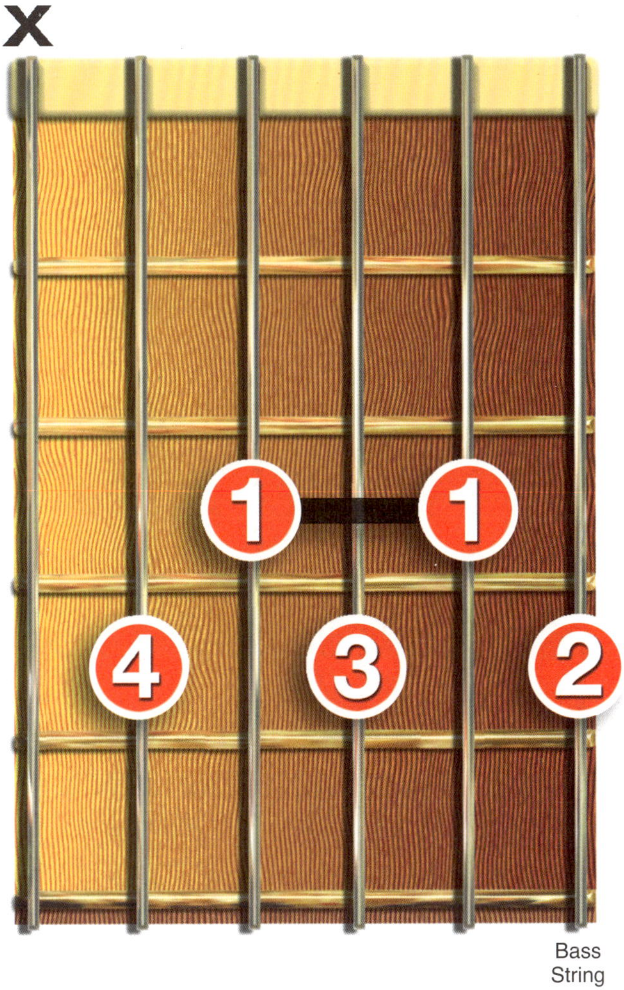

Chord Spelling

1st (A♭), 3rd (C), 5th (E♭), ♭7th (G♭), 9th (B♭)

FREE ACCESS on smartphones including iPhone & Android

Using any QR code app scan and **HEAR** the chord

G♯/A♭maj11

Major 11th

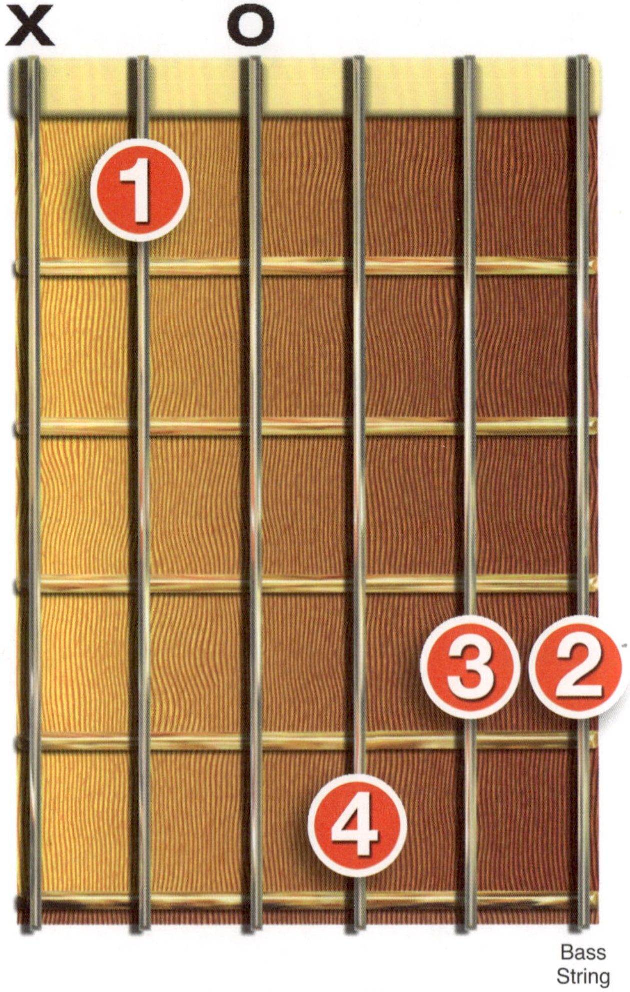
X
O
1
3
2
4
Bass String

Chord Spelling

1st (A♭), 3rd (C), 5th (E♭), 7th (G), 9th (B♭), 11th (D♭)

FREE ACCESS on smartphones including iPhone & Android

Using any QR code app scan and **HEAR** the chord

G♯/A♭maj13
Major 13th

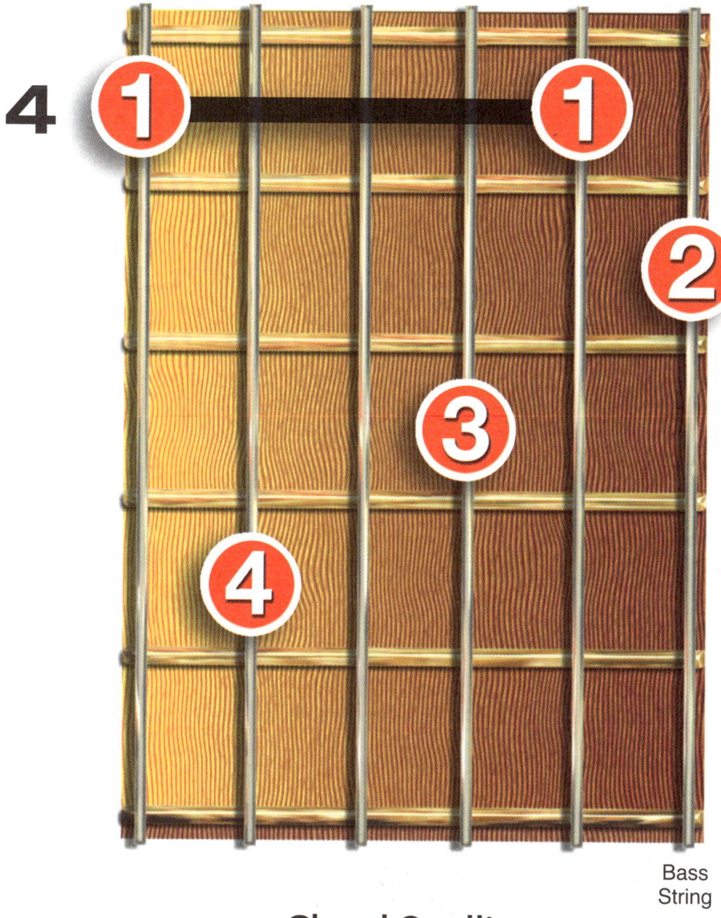

Chord Spelling

1st (A♭), 3rd (C), 5th (B♭), 7th (G), 9th (B♭), 11th (D♭), 13th (F)

FREE ACCESS on smartphones including iPhone & Android

Using any QR code app scan and **HEAR** the chord